THE LAST SPEAKER OF BEAR

the Last Speaker of Bear

My Encounters in the North

Lawrence Millman

TRINITY UNIVERSITY PRESS
SAN ANTONIO, TEXAS

Trinity University Press
San Antonio, Texas 78212

Book design by Anne Richmond Boston
Author photo by Deana Tempest Thomas
Cover illustration: iStock/Ekolara
Interior illustrations: iStock/leremy, iStock/pashonka, iStock/lantapix, iStock/Cattallina, iStock/Far700, iStock/KKstock, iStock/johnnylemon-seed, iStock/Triballium, iStockSvetlanaSoloveva

ISBN 978-1-59534-985-9 paperback
ISBN 978-1-59534-986-6 ebook

Trinity University Press strives to produce its books using methods and materials in an environmentally sensitive manner. We favor working with manufacturers that practice sustainable management of natural resources, produce paper using recycled stock, and manage forests with the best possible practices for people, biodiversity, and sustainability. The press is a member of the Green Press Initiative, a nonprofit program dedicated to supporting publishers in their efforts to reduce their impacts on endangered forests, climate change, and forest-dependent communities.

The paper used in this publication meets the minimum requirements of the American National Standard for Information Sciences—Permanence of Paper for Printed Library Materials, ANSI 39.48-1992.

CIP data on file at the Library of Congress

26 25 24 23 22 | 5 4 3 2 1

A man who keeps company with glaciers
comes to feel tolerably insignificant by and by.

— MARK TWAIN, *A Tramp Abroad*

They now advised me to stay at home, take a job and behave
myself. Which meant to me stay at home
and be dull and never do a thing you have not seen
thousands of others do in the exactly same way.

— PETER FREUCHEN, *Arctic Adventure*

I lie down in my little room where the moonlight
filters green through the small snowed-up windows.
Neither the walls of the hut nor the roof
can dispel my fancy that I am moonlight myself.

— CHRISTIANE RITTER, *A Woman in the Polar Night*

They say God made the world.
I think Kwakwadjec, Wolverine, made it. I *know* he did.
He put his lips to a muskrat's ass . . . and blew hard.
Very hard. Out came the world.

— INNU ELDER IN LABRADOR

CONTENTS

Preface ix

Encounters with Northern Natives 1
Encounters with Flora, Fauna, and Food 53
Encounters with Remote Places 99
Miscellaneous Encounters 167

Acknowledgments 215

My love affair with the North began when my parents took me on a fishing trip in northern Ontario. Our Cree guide reputedly talked to the fish, which, according to the other guides, was the reason his clients caught so many walleyes and northern pike. Once we got into his boat, I gazed at the myriad lines on his face and observed his bodily movements with such interest that my fishing line invariably got tangled up with my parents' lines.

Whenever one of us caught a fish, the Cree man would remove it from the hook, bring it closely to his lips, and whistle into its mouth. He also seemed to be communicating with the lake itself, now nodding and now shaking his head when he looked at it. Out of my parents' hearing, I asked him whether I could come and live with him so I could learn the ways of the Cree. He laughed. I was twelve years old at the time.

When I started venturing north on my own, I would find myself in a realm where Nature triumphs over the machinations of Man (Woman, too). Hurrah! I'd shout to myself, but then I would see evidence of climate change raising not just its ugly head, but its ugly body as well. After all, the North is warming two to three times faster than the rest of the planet. When will the last hurrah occur?

During my northern journeys, my only companion was often solitude, but no less often I would hang out with grizzled (the more grizzled, the better) facsimiles of the Cree fishing guide. These individuals would gratify me with traditional lore as well as tell me stories about their own past lives as hunter-gatherers. Sometimes I would hear what happened in the old days when they ran out of food.

Speaking of food, I often dined on time-honored victuals such as seal liver, *hákarl* (putrefied Icelandic shark's meat), *mataq* (raw whale blubber), caribou tongue, *igunaq* (fermented walrus meat), old sled dogs, and jerked whale meat. Such culinary items helped me conquer a linguistic hurdle. After all, food is a shared language, so even if I barely spoke the language of my dining partner, I could at least speak the language of the food we were eating. Hm-m-m, very nice seal nose, the expression on my face would say.

Given my variety of experiences, I decided to write a memoir about my time in the North. Easier said than done, for the narrative thread kept snapping under the weight of its numerous episodes. When the thread didn't snap, it would rush off in all sorts of strange directions without asking my permission. Meanwhile, chronology itself bowed out, saying, in effect, "Sorry, but this is not my bailiwick."

I ended up banishing the idea of a memoir. Instead, I decided to collect the snapped episodes and put them together in a book. Brevity may or may not be the soul of wit, but it happens to be the soul of this book.

Encounters
with
Northern Natives

ANNIE HENRY OF THE YUKON

Yukon Gwich'in elder Annie Henry had recently celebrated her hundredth birthday. To what did she attribute her longevity? "Eating country foods like caribou, moose, and berries," she told me. Then a euphoric smile seemed to sweep away all the cartographic lines on her face, and she added: "Laughter, too. In difficult times, you laugh, and then your troubles aren't so bad."

At the time I visited her, Annie was living in the town of Dawson City (pop. 1,500) after a hunter-gatherer lifetime spent in the Yukon backcountry. Although nearly blind, she was still beading moccasins. She could hardly walk, so one of her myriad grandchildren would push her wheelchair around Dawson several times a day. For she believed (as she told me) "the outdoor life is best."

At one point I noticed a bracket fungus, *Phellinus igniarius*, on the table next to her, and I mentioned that the Yupik in Alaska combined the ash of this fungus with tobacco leaves, creating the highly desirable item known as *iqmik*.

"We call it *metl'aat*," Annie told me, referring to the Gwich'in version of *iqmik*. Like the Yupik, the Gwich'in burn the polypore down to ash, then either mix the ash with tobacco or wrap a tobacco leaf around it, and then they begin chewing. The ash contains potassium, calcium, and magnesium, the combination of which accelerates the discharge of the tobacco's nicotine to the chewer's brain. The result? A nicotine high.

Annie's late husband, Joe, whom she'd been married to for eighty-two years, would sometimes mix the tobacco with ash soaked in whiskey or rum. Joe's nose had been broken several times due to run-ins with caribou, and Annie said his variant on chew-ash helped him much more than a visit to a doctor. She also said she rubbed the ashes (sans alcohol) into her own and other people's skin sores to ease the discomfort of those sores.

"How long have you chewed *metl'aat*?" I asked Annie.

"For about ninety years," she said, and laughed.

It was morel season, and the area around Dawson was filled with individuals collecting and selling this lucrative edible mushroom. I asked Annie what the Gwich'in word for morel was.

"We call them *yum-yums*," she said, laughing again.

It was now time for one of her wheelchair journeys around town, so I thanked Annie for her time and departed. She died a year after my visit. She and her husband, Joe, are memorialized in a bronze sculpture erected not far from the site of one of their backcountry cabins. Not surprisingly, this sculpture shows both of them laughing.

⎍⎍⎍⎍

SURVIVAL

I have a strange habit of losing whatever I happen to put on my feet. Once I tried to throw my boots across a river in a remote place in the Yukon so I could then wade across, and while I succeeded in throwing one boot across, the other landed squarely in the river, floated downstream, and disappeared.

Another time I climbed an icy mountain in Iceland, and upon reaching the summit, I decided to shake the snow off my crampons. I shook one of the crampons a bit too vigorously, and it flew off my boot and bounced down the mountain. As a result, my descent was more than a little difficult.

More recently, I was leading a nature walk outside Anchorage, Alaska, when—maybe to exhibit my expertise as an outdoorsman?—I tried to leap across a brook. Instead of landing on the other side, I landed in the middle of it, whereupon some of the folks on the walk cheered. One man shouted, "Terrific performance! Do it again!"

Needless to say, my boots were soaked from sole to shaft. That night I put them on the mat outside my motel room so they could get at least partially dry. The next morning, they were gone. Stolen, I assumed.

"I'll drive you to a store where you can buy some boots," said my friend Ted Mala, an Inupiat elder and director of traditional healing at the Alaska Native Medical Center in Anchorage. He also happened to be the son of Ray Mala, the star of the classic 1933 film *Eskimo*.

I warned Ted that my feet were so wide that I often had considerable difficulty finding boots or shoes that fit. He merely nodded.

Our first stop was a Sam's Club, where Ted was a member. Not surprisingly, none of the boots fit my feet. Then we visited a sporting goods store called Big Ray's. No luck. Then we went to an outdoor store whose products were designed for mountaineers, but it seemed that mountaineers don't have very wide feet.

In front of one store sat a drunk singing a ballad about a woman named Nellie, who "had hair all over her belly." I stopped to listen to the song, but Ted took my arm and we went into the store. No luck there, either.

"We're not going to find the right boot for me," I said.

"I'm a Native person," Ted replied, "and we haven't survived this long by giving up."

At last we visited a small shoe store next to a pile of oil drums (sometimes called the Alaska state flower due to their ubiquity). The owner, an Algerian man, seemed to understand my dilemma, and he retreated to the store's back room, then came out with boots that were a perfect fit. "I have very wide feet myself," he explained to me.

For his services, I treated Ted to dinner, and when I got back to my motel, I saw my other boots outside the door to my room. I learned later that the motel's cleaning woman thought I wanted them dried, so she took them and put them in the motel's dryer.

Now I possessed both an old and a new pair of boots. I put the two pairs together and looked at them. The older one reminded me of my own perpetual blunders, while the new one told me how northern indigenous people survive in habitats considerably more risky than urban Anchorage.

⊓⊔⊓⊔

COLLECTING LORE

It's a common belief that individuals who collect lore from indigenous people must hang out for a long time with their prospective informants before querying them about their customs. An academic ethnographer once told me that he emptied an Inuit family's honey bucket for two weeks before he asked members of that family for cultural lore. This, he stated, earned their trust.

On Disko Island, West Greenland, I was walking along a dirt road on the eastern side of the island when I heard these words: "Hey, *qallunaat* [white man]. Fuck you."

I saw a twentysomething Greenlander sitting on a boulder and drinking a can of Carlsberg beer. I replied: "Hey, *Kalaallit* [Greenlander]. Fuck you, too."

A huge grin appeared on the fellow's face. He offered me a can of Carlsberg, and I accepted it with a grin of my own.

In a short while, the fellow rode me back to his house on his ATV so I could meet his family (and doubtless drink more cans of Carlsberg). My seat on the ATV was very hard because a polar bear had recently eaten its foam rubber cushion.

Soon I was meeting members of his family. Two Carlsberg-drinking brothers, a mother who was a midwife, and a father who happened to be a traditional healer. The father offered me the following tidbits of information: the skin of a lemming makes a very nice bandage, an infusion of haircap moss will cure any sort of urinary infection you might have, a whip with a handle made from a polar bear's *oosik* (penis) will frighten away evil spirits if you swing it at them, and a tea made from mountain sorrel is a superb laxative.

Needless to say, I didn't empty a single honey bucket in order to obtain this lore . . . or any of the lore I describe in this book.

⌐⌐⌐⌐

ROSIE IQALLIJUQ, AN INTERVIEW

Nor did I need to empty a single chamber pot to interview an Inuit elder named Rosie Iqallijuq in Igloolik, Northwest Territories (now Nunavut), in 1995. She was at least ninety years old, and the wrinkles and clefts on her tattooed face were a written memorial to her long life.

Rosie asked me to climb into bed with her. Lest you think otherwise, she had no desire to sleep with me. According to Leah Otak, an Igloolik educator and cultural activist who helped me translate Rosie's Inuktitut, Rosie believed that if you want to communicate with someone, *really* communicate with them, you have to get very close to that person.

So it was that I climbed into bed with Rosie. What follows is an abbreviated version of the interview I had with her.

Q: *You're probably the last living person who met explorers Knud Rasmussen and Peter Freuchen when they passed through Repulse Bay on the Fifth Thule Expedition.*

A: This was more than seventy years ago. They were both very kind *qallunaat* (white men). I made drawings of Inuit clothes, both men's and women's clothes, for Mr. Rasmussen, and they appeared in one of his books. My drawings look really messed up in the book.

Q: *Messing up one's work is a specialty of publishers. So tell me about Peter Freuchen.*

A: He was so tall, we called him Piitarjuaq. That means Big Peter. He was big in more ways than one . . . [Here Rosie's face burst into a smile that seemed to consume all of her face's tattoos.]

Q: *No need to tell me any more. I understand. So when you were living in Repulse Bay, did you meet the trader George Washington Cleveland?*

A: Yes. He had the largest nose of any person in the Arctic.

Q: *Did you call him Big Nose?*

A: *Nakka!* That would have been wrong, for some people thought he was an *angakok* [shaman].

Q: *An ex-whaler from the United States was an angakok?*

A: He had false teeth. My people had never seen false teeth before, so they thought he could make magic, like an *angakok*. And if they didn't trade with him, they thought he would put a curse on

them. That's why he kept taking out his false teeth
. . . so they would trade with him.

Q: *I've heard Mr. Cleveland had three Inuit wives.*

A: That's not a lot. In Chesterfield Inlet, where I grew
up, there was a man who had six wives. Such men
often shared their wives with *nuliaqati* [men in need
of sex].

Q: *Were there any sexual taboos when you were growing
up?*

A: My people thought that someone who wasn't
having sex with other people must be having sex
with an animal, and sex with an animal would
always make you sick. You could get well only by
going to see an *angakok*, and if you confessed to
him you just had sex with a sled dog or a caribou,
he would cure you of the sickness.

Q: *Any other taboos you can tell me about?*

A: The return of the sun after such a long period of
darkness—it was a really important time for us,
so it was taboo to play string games when it was
returning.

Q: *I don't understand. Why couldn't you play string
games?*

A: Because we thought the sun might get tangled
     in the strings. Of course, we now know that this
     would never happen.

Q: *I see you have some caribou meat on your bedside table.*
     What if you didn't have anything to eat in the old days?

A: My first mother-in-law ate her husband right
     after he died. She said he was so shrunken, there
     wasn't much meat on him. Then I knew a woman
     named Ataguttaaluk who ate her children and her
     husband after they starved. Our high school is
     named after her.

Q: *And what about the times you didn't have any food*
     yourself?

A: When I was a young girl, I once lived for a
     month on only three fish. This wasn't much fun.
     But starvation told us that being alive is very
     important . . .

This statement seemed like a fitting conclusion to
our interview. I thanked Rosie for her time and got up
from her bed.

⊓⊔⊓⊔

CREE FIRE MAKING

A large robust man, Cree elder Jimmy Mianscum was seventy-five years old, but he didn't look any older than fifty. He also had the step of a man half his age. A lifetime in the bush seemed to have preserved him from the worst aspects of time's ravages.

One day Jimmy took me in his ATV to a mixed grove of poplar, birch, and black spruce several miles from his home in the village of Oujé-Bougoumou in northern Quebec. Beneath one of the spruce trees, he placed a bear trap. Then he began smearing "beaver juice" over the tree's bark. This is a yellowish secretion from the castor scent glands situated near a beaver's anal opening and is used by beavers to mark their territory.

Black bears find beaver juice irresistible, Jimmy told me. So irresistible, in fact, that they're completely oblivious to the trap on the ground until they happen to step into it.

Once he got a bear, he would kill it and skin it, then sell the pelt to the Hudson Bay Company while saving the meat for his family. The claws were good luck charms, so he kept them until the local Pentecostal pastor railed at him, saying that such diabolical things could land him in hell.

On a nearby birch stump, I pointed to several tinder polypores (*Fomes fomentarius*). Calling this fungus by its Cree name, *upsagan*, Jimmy said the local Cree had traditionally used it as a fire starter. He also told me about another, extremely important use of *upsagans*. Once they were smoldering, they could be used as a mosquito smudge.

As mosquitoes were swarming around us, I took a smoldering *upsagan* that Jimmy had ignited and waved it around me, and since the mosquitoes couldn't detect the carbon dioxide of my exhalations, they flew away. Not only did smoldering fungus work better than a store-bought repellent like DEET, but it was far healthier for the user, too.

The Oujé-Bougoumou Cree depended on *upsagans* for fire-starting until the middle years of the twentieth century, and then matches took over.

"But matches have their drawbacks," Jimmy observed. "You can't use the same match more than once, but you can use the same *upsagan* repeatedly. All you need to do is douse it with water, then scrape off the charred area."

Having made a fire with an *upsagan*, he now began performing a *mitunsaawaakan* (scapula divination). This surprised me, for I assumed such rituals had died out in the Canadian North. After all, most people can simply visit a grocery store and purchase their prey rather than divine that prey's whereabouts with a shoulder bone.

Jimmy now tied the shoulder bone of an arctic hare to the end of a stick and held it over the fire, with the bone's lateral process facing upward.

"Are you using a hare's shoulder bone because you'd be hunting arctic hares?" I asked.

He shook his head. "Hare shoulder bones 'speak' for any animal I might be hunting," he said, his face glistening in the sun like polished bronze.

After several minutes, there were cracks only on the edges of the scapula. This showed that we'd be forced to make a long hike and even then we might not find our game, so the scapula was telling us to remain in our camp.

Jimmy also made the following observations: If the scapula hardly darkens at all, that would mean bad luck—maybe you'd get lost while searching for your prey. A completely blackened scapula meant bad weather . . . so bad that there would be no point in leaving camp.

And if the scapula had a large char mark in the middle, the prey would be very close to one's camp.

I asked him whether the divination process really worked.

"Well, we starved a lot in the old days," he observed with a grin.

⊓⊔⊓⊔

DREAMS

One morning I was wandering around the Labrador Innu village of Sheshatshiu, alternately searching for tradition-bound individuals and swatting at black flies. At one point, an elder approached me and said, "Last night I dreamed I would meet you. I dreamed you'd be coming to my house today."

I gathered the man had spent much of the morning trying to track me down. Which wouldn't have been easy, given his lame, arthritic hobble. But Innu custom required him to invite me to his house even if he hated my guts. After all, he had dreamed about doing so.

I accepted the invitation, and the fellow turned out to be just the sort of person I was looking for. Not only did he know old stories, but he knew cures, too. I'll always cherish his backwoods remedy for a serious toothache: put a little gunpowder on the offending tooth, then a match to that tooth, and BANG! the toothache's gone.

I joined this elder in his jerry-built, government issue house; a dwelling that would have been a seamless fit in a Third World slum. Soon we were talking about dreams, which are (or were) an essential part of Innu life.

"I'll tell you something," my host informed me. "A person is born empty. Dreams fill him. It's just like you've got a Ski-Doo. A Ski-Doo can't go anywhere unless it's filled with petrol."

I seldom have dreams myself. Or, if I do, I can hardly remember them. "What about a person who doesn't have dreams?" I inquired.

"That person would be no better than a *bokageesh*," the man replied. Which means a black fly.

During the next few days, I thought of myself as a *bokageesh*. Thus I would shout, "Take that, *sister*!" when I swatted at the black flies that landed on me, for it's the female rather than the male black flies that delight in sucking out one's blood.

ᒧᒧᒧᒧ

KILLING STORIES

In Saqqaq, West Greenland, I was talking with a local woman dressed in sealskin trousers, a quilted jacket, and a worsted cap. While we talked, she observed the not uncommon Greenlandic habit of chewing used coffee grounds as if they were tobacco. At one point, I happened to mention that ethnographers in Greenland have collected more stories from men than from women.

"Women know just as many stories as men," she informed me, "but we don't tell them to *qallunaat* [white people] like you all the time. Because if you tell a story too often, you might injure it, even kill it."

This observation made me hesitant to ask her for a story. Once she noticed the look on my face, the woman, whose name was Kanneyak (Little Sculpin), said, "I know a very good *oqalualat* [old story]. If I tell it to you, I don't think I'll hurt it . . ."

She now told me this story, her fingers moving mesmerically as she talked:

There was once an old woman who couldn't even chew *kamiks* (soft sealskin boots) anymore, so her family left her to starve on an island. She grew very hungry, and all she could find to eat on the island were some insects.

"I'm not going to eat these creatures," she said. "I am old, and perhaps they are young. Perhaps even a few are children. I would rather starve than eat them . . ."

A short while later, a fox appeared out of nowhere and started nibbling on her just like it was taking off her clothes. Soon it had nibbled off all her old skin. And what lay beneath that old skin was a pretty young woman. For the grateful insects had told their friend the fox to save the old woman from starving.

The next summer the woman's family visited the island where they had left her. They did not find her body or even her bones. For she had gone to live with the insects. It's said that she had married a very handsome bumblebee she'd fallen in love with.

"That's the *oqalualat*," remarked the woman, and then she uttered a few words in Greenlandic that I wasn't able to follow. I asked her what she had just said.

"I asked the *oqalualat* if I injured it by telling it to you," she replied, grabbing some more used coffee grounds, "and it told me, 'Not at all.'"

HUDSON

In 1611, a mutinous crew dumped explorer Henry Hudson as well as his son and several loyal crew members into a small boat in James Bay. What became of Hudson is conjecture. Did he freeze to death? Starve to death? Was he killed by Huron First Nation people who didn't appreciate a white man in their territory? Did he try to make it back to England and somehow end up dying in Svalbard?

As for myself, I thought Hudson might have ended up near the Cree village of Wemindji in James Bay. For that's where Hudson Bay's currents would have taken his small boat from the probable marooning site. So it was that I went to Wemindji and began asking Cree elders if they know any stories about a white man named Henry Hudson.

One of the elders informed me that Hudson had been a great man for the ladies. He would walk up to a woman and say, "Shall we?" Minutes later, she would be hugging him. He was a really handsome man, the fellow said.

Here was oral lore that would seem to indicate Henry Hudson had indeed come ashore in these parts.

Likewise oral lore that indicated his desire to court indigenous women. I wondered if there might be some Cree around today who had the explorer's blood flowing in their veins.

"No mystery has a deeper shadow than that which hangs over the fate of Hudson," one chronicler wrote, and now I thought I might be close to solving that mystery.

"How did you learn about Hudson's interest in women?" I asked the elder excitedly. "Maybe from talking to elders in your youth?"

"Not at all. I learned about his interest in women from watching a movie called *The Magnificent Obsession*," he replied.

It was then that I realized he'd been telling me about Rock Hudson, not Henry . . .

ᴫᴫᴫ

AULD LANG SYNE

During the summer, vast armadas of Winnebagos from Alaska swagger and lurch across the Canadian border and clog the streets of Dawson City in Canada's Yukon Territory.

I was seated on a bench in Dawson and talking with a Vuntut Gwich'in elder when a Winnebago paused in front of us while its driver fingered his iDevice. The music coming out of the Winnebago's audio system inspired my companion to tell me this story:

Fifty or so years ago, the elder had just arrived with a pile of muskrat furs at the Hudson Bay Company trading post at Fort Rampart in the Yukon. All of a sudden, he heard this loud, wailing sound. What could that sound be? Sled dogs in agony? No, he could identify whining, howling, screaming sled dogs. Could the sound be a dying person lamenting the loss of his or her life?

"I was so frightened that I ran into the bush, leaving my furs behind," the Gwich'in man said.

Eventually, he decided to brave it out, so he walked toward the trading post. The closer he got, the louder the wailing became. When he opened the door, the wailing, accompanied by a raucous drone, dramatically increased in its magnitude.

Then he saw the trader, a Scotsman dressed in kilts, walking back and forth and playing the bagpipes.

"You know what tune the fellow was playing on those bagpipes?" the Gwich'in man said. "The same tune that's coming out of that Winnebago—'Auld Lang Syne.'"

At virtually the same moment he uttered these words, the Winnebago drove off.

⌐⌐⌐⌐

AN EXPERT MECHANIC

I was standing on the airstrip in Upernavik, West Greenland, when a helicopter landed but couldn't take off because its engine had somehow gone awry. The Danish pilot tinkered with it, tinkered with it some more, and gave up. Then an elderly Greenlandic man asked the pilot whether he could try to fix the engine. Actually, he asked whether he could "play with the engine."

"Play with it all you like," the pilot said, and shrugged. Then he turned to me and said, "Whatever that old guy does to the engine can't make it any worse than it already is."

After half an hour or so, the Greenlander said, in Danish, "*Alt er godt nu.*" Which means the engine is fixed now. The pilot's astonished expression remained on his face even as he raised the chopper into the air.

I asked the elder whether he'd ever fixed a helicopter engine before. He shook his head. He'd fixed a few outboard motors, he said, but never a helicopter engine. Then how, I asked, had he succeeded in fixing this one?

He pointed to his head and tapped it.

For he lived in the literal Stone Age (the Greenlandic word for stone, *ujurak*, is also the word for earth), where, if you don't know how to improvise, you don't survive.

᠅

LONGEVITY

In Igloolik, Nunavut, I once spent several nights sleeping on the floor of an Inuit couple's cabin where the water came from melted snow and the temperature hovered only a few degrees above freezing.

The biggest problem was not the living quarters but the couple's six-year-old daughter. She tipped over chamber pots, kicked around prized edibles like seal flippers, and—perhaps because of the negative effect of my race on hers—smilingly called me an *inuittuniq* (cannibal). Her behavior made me think of the French philosopher Denis Diderot's well-known epigram: "All children are essentially criminals."

At last I told the mother that she should do something to control the little brat, though I used the word *niviarsiaq* (girl), not brat. The mother shook her head vigorously. The girl's grandmother had died the day before she was born, and the old woman's *isuma* (spirit) had immediately entered the little girl.

"Why does that stop you from spanking her?" I said casually, as if being in possession of another person's *isuma* was an everyday occurrence.

"My mother is inside my daughter," the woman told me, "and if I spanked my daughter, I would also be spanking my mother." A pause. "You don't spank your mothers in America, do you?"

"Very seldom," I replied, even as the little girl was rubbing seal grease onto my trouser leg.

When a Danish economic development officer offered me a room in his modern dwelling, I eagerly accepted, then thanked my former hosts for their hospitality. As I was leaving the cabin, the girl gave me a grumpy look, one that seemed to say, "You do not appreciate my longevity."

⌐⌐⌐⌐

STRANGERS ON THE TUNDRA

On a visit to Baker Lake, Nunavut, I happened to meet an Inuk who told me he'd observed the Holy Trinity walking on the tundra in the dead of winter forty or so years ago. Needless to say, I was surprised to hear this, and I jokingly asked him if he might have been drunk at the time.

"I wasn't drunk or—what's the new word?—*ujarak* [stoned]," he said. "I could see them as clearly as I see you right now."

"Okay, but how were they dressed? In the thin garb of the Holy Land?"

"The Father and the Son were dressed in caribou hide clothes, just as we were dressed. But the Holy Ghost, he wasn't wearing anything except a badly worn rabbit skin hat."

"He must have been frozen solid."

"Ghosts can't freeze. I bet that's as true in your country as it is here. Anyway, my wife and I invited these strangers into our snow house for some tea and biscuits, but they paid no attention to us. It was like we didn't exist. They went on walking, and then they disappeared."

"Perhaps *they* didn't exist."

"If they didn't exist, then why were our sled dogs barking and howling at them? Barking and howling at them just like they were *qallupilluit* [evil spirits]. Maybe they were *qallupilluit*, too . . ."

⊓⊔⊓⊔

AN ENCOUNTER WITH A *QIVITTOQ*

As we were hiking along a peninsula south of Igaliku in West Greenland, my Inuit guide said we should avoid a person named Anda at all costs, and then he told about this unusual fellow:

Some years ago, this Anda had gone seal hunting with several of his friends. They were all drunk, and their boat ended up ramming an ice floe. Only Anda survived the capsizing. Being the oldest of the party, he felt responsible for the tragedy. Indeed, such was his shame that he couldn't live with his people anymore. Thus, he went to live in the remote place directly ahead of us and became a *qivittoq*.

"What's a *qivittoq*?" I asked my guide.

"Something like a flying *nanoq* [polar bear]," my guide said. "The *qivittoq* will fly into a village, grab a person, and eat him. Or he'll fly the person back to his home, dry him, and eat him later."

Rather than put me off, this description of Anda made me eager to meet him. My guide shrugged, as if to say, "Okay, but I warned you." Hiking on, we arrived at a nearby gulley that wasn't visible until we reached the edge. Then we ventured down that gulley.

All at once I saw a man with wrinkled parchment skin squatting in front of a haphazard-looking stone dwelling. Every few feet, my guide called out "we are friendly, we are friendly" in Greenlandic. There was no reply. At last we were standing only a few feet away from Anda. He gazed at us with no discernible interest. He was dressed entirely in sealskins so rank that mosquitoes avoided him. From inside the hovel of stones wafted the smell of petrified sweat.

"*Qaqqislunga qatangajualaq*," my guide whispered. Which means "He has not wiped off his snot in many years."

Slowly Anda opened his mouth to reveal a long tooth extending like a fang from his upper jaw. He didn't seem eager to eat either of us. Quite the contrary. He asked us for food in a voice that seemed to be cracking from disuse.

My guide gave him some dried whale meat, and I gave him several Cliff bars.

After receiving these gifts, Anda played host and offered us a thermos of cold tea. Drink, he instructed us. We drank straight from the thermos (Anda seemed to have no cups) even as I wondered what diseases unknown to medical science I might pick up from a man capable of turning into a polar bear. The tea tasted bitter and caustic, yet custom decreed that we shouldn't offend him by spitting it out.

My guide asked our hermit host how he had managed to get his tea, and Anda said his son Soren visited him two or three times a year, bringing him supplies such as tea, sugar, flour, and seal meat, along with batteries for his tape recorder.

"Tape recorder?" I asked with a look of surprise on my face.

Anda nodded and inserted a cassette of music by the Greenlandic pop group Seqikaq (Good for Nothings) into this recorder, and we were treated to a scratchy, almost unlistenable sound. Either the tape heads on the recorder hadn't been cleaned in a long time or the tape itself was beyond repair.

Both my guide and I cringed at the sound. We cringed even more when Anda offered each of us what looked like thousand-year-old doughnuts.

Anda seemed to take our cringes seriously. An expression of agony appeared on his face. "Go away! Leave me with my shame!" he shouted at us.

And so we left him. Ten or so minutes later, I turned around, and my last glimpse of the so called *qivittoq* was of a small elderly man squatting beside his stone dwelling in apparent contentment.

⌐⌐⌐⌐

SUPPORTING ART

I was heading toward the only store in the village of Ittoqqortoormiit, East Greenland, when a local man sprang out of an apparent nowhere and hugged me, saying, "*Qanoq ippit, ilannaaq?*" (How are you, my friend?)

I'd felt a stab in my chest, for the fellow had been wearing a crucifix around his neck and that crucifix had gouged me. I also detected the scent of alcohol wafting from the wearer of the crucifix. It seemed to emanate not so much from his mouth as from his entire body.

"That crucifix is a dangerous weapon," I told him. And I rubbed my chest to provide evidence of this fact.

Not only did the Greenlander take off the weapon in question, but he flung it into a nearby ditch. This didn't prove he wasn't a local minister. After all, he could have simply been a drunken one. Then the fellow hugged me again. "Buy me some alcohol, or I'll die," he proclaimed, his swollen, coddled-egg eyes beseeching me.

My race had already poisoned natives of the North with vast amounts of alcohol. What should I do now? Continue with the poisoning? Or maybe play the part of a crucifix wearer myself and say, "Drinking is bad for your soul . . . unless you're drinking the blood of Jesus."

All at once I noticed a carving of a polar bear sticking out of the man's pocket. "Did you carve that *nanuk*?" I asked.

He nodded. "I sell to you for fifty kroner," he said.

I gave the fellow a hundred Danish kroner, and he headed off with a blissful smile on his face.

As I continued walking toward the market, I consoled myself with the thought that I seemed to be supporting Greenlandic art. For a new polar bear or walrus carving would probably greet the world in a few days.

ᴨᴜᴨᴨ

A GREENLANDIC SOCCER MATCH

I pitched my tent just outside the village of Igaliku in West Greenland, and as I was making coffee, I received an invitation of sorts. A Greenlandic kid who seemed no older than eleven or twelve kicked a soccer ball in my direction with a big smile on his face.

Soon we adjourned to the nearby soccer field, which turned out to be thick with chamomile. I probably should have made myself some tea on the spot, for chamomile tea is very soothing and might have helped me deal with the violence of Greenlandic soccer.

It wasn't long before we were joined by two other kids who were roughly the same age, and a match was suggested. Since none of the kids showed any enthusiasm for being on my side, I ended up playing against all three of them, a White Man vastly outnumbered by the Natives.

Right away I learned that my opponents were just as inclined to kick me as the ball. One of them would block me out, another would bash away at my shins, and the third would drive the ball triumphantly to the goal. Or all three would dedicate themselves to bashing my shins, seemingly forgetting about the ball.

The match's underlying message seemed to be "Off the White Guy." The contemporary world of getting and spending may be his, but now we've got him on the holy ground of our soccer field, and we're the ones in charge.

After the so-called match came to an end (the Greenlandic kids won it, of course), one of my opponents called me a lousy Dane. I told him I was a lousy American, not a lousy Dane. He looked puzzled, for he'd probably never seen an American except on television.

Back at my tent I considered an aggressive return match in which I turned these kids into something akin to Inuit gelatin. But then I remembered the evils of the island's Danish colonization—for example, the infamous G60 policy, which forcibly relocated Greenlanders from their small, traditional villages to the burgeoning, unhealthy capital of Nuuk—and I realized the version of Greenlandic soccer I'd just participated in had been an appropriate act of revenge.

⊓⊔⊓⊔

LATE TO SCHOOL

In winter 1941, several Inuit on the Belcher Islands in Hudson Bay went on a rampage after being converted to Christianity. Non-Christians, they assumed, were Satan and should be disposed of. In response to various acts of violence toward putative Satans, the Canadian government exiled the assailants to the mainland village of Moose Factory in northern Ontario.

In Moose Factory, I met with several Cree elders who remembered the Belcher Island Inuit.

"They were always smiling," one man told me.

"At first we thought they would kill us," another said, "but then we realized they were just like us."

"They didn't know our language, and we didn't know theirs," an elder named John Trapper observed.

Here I might mention the fact that the missionaries who were christening the Cree in the nineteenth and early twentieth centuries couldn't pronounce Cree names, so they gave them eminently pronounceable English surnames like Trapper, Hunter, Shotgun, Blacksmith, and Bearskin.

That evening John Trapper showed up at the guesthouse where I was staying. "There's something I couldn't talk about in front of the others," he said. "It's too . . . *strong.*"

He was attending Bishop Horden residential school, he told me, and one morning he was walking to school (he was lodged in a separate compound from the actual school) when he happened to see Akeenik, one of the Belcher Inuit, behind the fence at the Royal Canadian Mounted Police compound.

Akeenik was "a new girl in town," John said. He wandered over to her, and she met him on the other side of the fence.

"She spoke only Inuit, and I spoke only Cree and a little English," he told me, "but we still tried to talk to each other. We spent a lot of time laughing because we couldn't understand a word the other was saying. Then we tried to communicate with gestures, and that didn't work, either. So we ended up laughing again."

He arrived so late to school that his teacher, an Anglican minister, was furious with him. So furious that he began clubbing one of John's hands with a birch rod. He clubbed it both repeatedly and hard. *Very* hard.

When John cried out in Cree rather than English, his teacher clubbed John's hand some more, since kids in the school weren't allowed to speak their own language.

"Almost seventy years later," John told me, pointing to his left hand, "I still have very little feeling in this hand."

The expression on his bone-ridged, heavy-jawed face was now so painful that the minister's assault might have happened only a few minutes ago. Was it my imagination, or did I see tears in his eyes?

ᒪᒪᒪ

THE LAST WINDIGO

In the Canadian North, a tall, remarkably emaciated figure with a rank odor, lips eaten away to expose wildly crooked teeth, and a hyperextended tongue once had the habit of tottering into a bush camp. Often drooling blood, this figure would look eagerly at one or more of the camp's inhabitants. You might think those inhabitants would quickly give the visitor a chunk of moose or caribou meat. Not at all, for they themselves were its meat.

The figure in question was a windigo (alternate spellings: weendigo, weetigo, and wendigo), a person who, in the absence of food, would eat members of his own species. Someone who engaged in this cannibalistic act automatically became a windigo. In other words, once you ate another person, you'd henceforth depend on other people as your cuisine.

Windigos departed from their former human morphology. Some possessed dramatically protruding ribs, some had beards around their hearts, and some had cloven feet and hooves. A missionary in the late nineteenth century described Satan's appearances to a Cree man. "We have Satans here, sir," the man said. "We call them windigos."

Like the passenger pigeon, the Tasmanian tiger, and the dodo, windigos are probably extinct now. For starvation itself has become a thing of the past among northern indigenous people. After all, a person's hunger can be alleviated by a visit to a local market.

According to a Cree elder I met in Moose Factory, the last windigo died in 1962. Not having eaten a human being in quite a while, it was famished, so it decided to stand in front of the train that traveled between Las Pas and Churchill, Manitoba. It figured this act would cause the train to come to an abrupt halt, whereupon it would have a veritable banquet of passengers at its disposal.

Obviously, this windigo knew nothing about the power of a speeding locomotive. Or perhaps it was overly besotted by its own seemingly supernatural powers. In any event, the train didn't stop but simply ran down the windigo and continued its journey to Churchill.

"I think it's really a shame there aren't any more windigos," the elder said after telling me about this fatal accident. "When they were here, we paid more attention to the world around us. We listened to every sound, every crackling in the bush. We studied every movement closely. This was not only because we were hunters looking for game, but also because we didn't want to become game ourselves."

⎍⎍⎍

THE LAST SPEAKER OF BEAR

I was talking on the phone with Uinipapeu Rich, an acquaintance in the Labrador Innu village of Utshimassits. At one point in our conversation, he happened to mention a local elder who spoke bear. I became excited. So excited that I decided to meet the speaker of this obscure language.

A week later, I flew to Goose Bay, Labrador, then hopped the mail flight to Utshimassits. Once it left Goose (as it's commonly called), our piston-engine plane began to take a beating from the elements. Buffeted like a shuttlecock in the turbulent air, it got only as far as the coastal village of Makkovik before it ran out of fuel. The only fuel in Makkovik was helicopter fuel, which requires a filter. As there was no filter in Makkovik, a special plane had to fly one in from Goose. Bad weather in Goose prevented the filter from being flown in, so the pilot, the two other passengers, and I had to spend the night in Makkovik.

The next day the plane, having been refueled, took off again. In a short while, sleet, snow, and ice pellets rendered the windshield wipers useless, forcing the pilot to roll down a window and stick out his head to determine where we happened to be going. We seemed to be flying into a giant platter of béchamel sauce. The pilot was obliged to make a forced landing in Hopedale, which was two villages up the coast from Makkovik. The béchamel sauce persisted for another day, so the pilot, another passenger, and I were obliged to spend a night in Hopedale.

At last the plane reached Utshimassits, where I was greeted by Uinipapeu. "Too bad you didn't get here earlier," he said. "The elder I told you about died yesterday from a heart attack. He was probably the last of our people to speak bear."

I offered my condolences. I also tried to conceal my disappointment by asking Uinipapeu if he knew any words—or at least grunts—of the bear language himself.

"Only a few, but I would speak them so badly that it would be an insult to bears."

"Then maybe you could just give me some idea of what a person might say to a bear?" I asked.

"He would call the bear Grandfather because it was so wise, then he would ask it this question: 'My family is very hungry, so would it be okay if I kill you, Grandfather?' 'Yes,' the bear would tell him, 'I don't mind if you kill me, but you'll have to smoke a pipe with me after you've done so . . .'"

"How can a dead bear smoke a pipe?" I interrupted.

"Because only the bear's flesh is dead. Its spirit is still alive. Anyway, the speaker would tell the bear that he'd be very glad to smoke a pipe with it. In the old days, we used to have special pipes for bears."

I asked Uinipapeu what would happen if a hunter killed a bear and didn't ask the bear's permission first or smoke a pipe with the deceased animal.

"This would make the bear's spirit really angry. It would tell other bears not to give themselves to the hunter. Then the hunter would never be able to kill another bear."

"I've heard that a bear's skull is very important."

"In the old days, yes. First, we would cook the bear's brains in its skull, and a person who ate the brains would have the strength and courage of a bear. Then we would put the skull on the branch of a tree to protect our camps. No harm could come to us if we did that."

I still wanted to hear what the language of bears sounded like. "So nobody speaks even a few words of bear now?" I asked.

He shook his head. "Today we just kill bears, and we don't even smoke a pipe with them after we kill them."

We now observed a moment of silence that felt like an act of reverence to a dead language.

ᘛᘚ

Encounters
with
Flora, Fauna, and Food

FLYING IN CHUKOTKA

In the remote village of Uelen in Siberia's Chukotka District, there aren't many restaurants. No take-outs or curbside deliveries, either. So one day I went foraging for mushrooms on the tundra, and I soon collected enough scaber stalks (*Leccinum scabrum*) to feed me for several days, assuming I accompanied them with something like seal or walrus blubber. For mushrooms require more calories to digest than they contain, so it's a good idea to eat a fatty food along with them.

On another day I went foraging with a local schoolteacher, Umqy, whose name meant "Polar Bear," and we happened on a fruiting of fly agarics (*Amanita muscaria*), a mushroom that the Chukchi call *wapak*. This red-capped, psychoactive species with rings of white warts on its cap is iconic, appearing in *Alice in Wonderland* as well as on postcards and stoner websites.

Traditionally, the Chukchi ate *wapaks* in order to get in touch with their ancestors. Upon doing so, they would ask those ancestors about (for example) how they could get rid of the viral infection afflicting their reindeer or whether a certain woman would make a decent wife.

"With a *wapak*, you don't need a ticket or a boarding pass," Umqy said, with a grin on his face. For the mushroom typically makes you feel like you're flying.

Here I should mention that Chukchi who ate *wapaks* in Stalinist times were regarded as enemies of the state. After all, they were engaged in a highly individual rather than a communal act. Reputedly, those who ate *wapaks* were forced onto a plane, and once the plane was in the air, the cargo door would be flung open.

"You say you can fly," a Stalinist henchman would announce. "Okay, then fly." Whereupon he would push his victims out of the plane.

So planted in their genes are such unpleasant incidents from the Soviet era that many Chukchi are reluctant to talk about cultural matters with Russians even today. We have no *wapaks* in our area, a Chukchi elder told a Russian ethnographer of my acquaintance. But since I wasn't Russian, Umqy had no problem sharing his lore with me. For instance, he gave me the following instructions on how to pick a *wapak*:

You should be extremely careful with the cap. If you damage it, you might end up with some sort of head injury. If you remove the warts from the cap, you might end up losing all your hair. And if you injure the stem, something unpleasant will happen to one of your legs.

"How unpleasant?" I asked.

"The leg might need to be amputated," he replied.

I'd heard that in earlier times only a shaman was allowed to eat the mushroom, and then his followers would drink his urine. For muscimol—the primary trip-taking alkaloid in *A. muscaria*—passes through a person's system more or less unaltered.

I asked Umqy if he'd ever drunk the urine of a shaman.

"We hardly have any shamans now," he told me. "But I once drank some of my own *mocha* (piss) after I ate a few *wapaks*. I didn't fly very far, though."

I decided to eat some *wapaks* myself. So, being extremely careful not to damage them, I gathered a few mushrooms and dried them. That night Umqy told me I had to bare my naked buttocks to the moon just before I ate them. If I didn't, I would suffer from a prolonged bout of bad luck. When I lowered my trousers and raised my buttocks, he and a few of his friends burst into riotous laughter.

"We've made a joke on you," Umqy said.

"*Luna ne naplevat' na tvoyu zadnitsu!*" one of his friends said, and guffawed. Which means "the moon doesn't give a damn about your ass" in Russian.

How did I feel after eating the mushroom? As it happened, I didn't fly off to visit my own ancestors, wherever they happened to be, but I did feel upbeat, an emotion somewhat unusual for my typically downbeat self. In fact, I felt so upbeat that I joined the other individuals in laughing at the sight of my naked buttocks.

Let me conclude by saying that most Chukchi don't eat *wapaks* nowadays. Instead, they drink vodka, plenty of it. I can imagine their ancestors feeling very lonely, with almost no one visiting them anymore.

⊓⊔⊓⊔

A GRIZZLY ENCOUNTER

Some years ago, I went in search of a grizzly bear. Not just any grizzly bear, mind you. I hoped to find a rare white color variation of the ordinary brown grizzly that inhabits the Kootenay Mountains of eastern British Columbia. There are probably no more than a hundred of these white grizzlies in existence.

Grizzlies, white or otherwise, like to dine on marmots, so I started my search in the Dennis Creek watershed, a common marmot hangout. Or I should say *we* started our search, for I was accompanied by my photographer friend David, who was eager to document a white grizzly sighting. That David could carry fifty pounds of photographic equipment on his back over rough terrain was a tribute to his physical fitness.

We followed the Dennis Creek Trail for a mile or so, then climbed up a steep slope pockmarked by marmot burrows. Several of these burrows looked like they'd been excavated by foraging bears, though not very recently. After much huffing and puffing, we reached a narrow alpine ridge, where we could scrutinize the surrounding slopes for possible white grizzly activity. David set up his tripod, while I walked along the ridge, looking for signs of our quarry.

All of a sudden I saw a pale speck in the distance. My pulse accelerated. Could that speck be one of the elusive white grizzlies? I quickly raised my binoculars to my eyes. Whereupon I discovered that I was gazing at a large quartz boulder.

An hour later, I saw another white speck. This one was moving, an activity totally out of character for a boulder. "Come here, quick," I shouted at David. "I see a white grizzly on a ridge."

David grabbed his tripod and ran over to where I was standing. I pointed. He lifted up his binoculars, then said, "It's a truck on a logging road." His voice had a somewhat condescending tone.

For the next few days, we didn't even see a remote facsimile of a white grizzly. Then at five a.m. on the morning of our last day, I clambered half-asleep from our tent to answer nature's call. While I was doing so, I noticed that I was standing between a white grizzly mom and her two cubs. She was perhaps a hundred feet away, and her cubs were no more than fifty feet away.

What do wilderness guidebooks tell you to do in a situation like this? I asked myself. Abort answering the call in question and run? Back up while still answering the call? Curl up into a sodden ball?

Before I had time to decide, the mother bear stood up on her hind legs, and her ears wiggled in concentration. Then all at once she began quickly running up the nearest slope, as if she was terrified by what she'd just witnessed. A very strange act on her part: mother bears almost never abandon their cubs like this. The cubs circumvented me and followed her up the slope.

I now dashed back to the tent. "Wake up, white grizzlies are out there!" I yelled at David. There was no response, so I shook him forcibly, and at last he woke up. I told him about the white grizzlies, but it took so long for him to get his camera equipment together and launch himself from the tent that by the time we arrived where I'd been only minutes before, the bears were no more than tiny white pinpricks above us.

Over coffee, I described my encounter with a fair degree of exactitude.

"On the one hand, I've missed a golden opportunity to get some good photos," David remarked, "but on the other hand, I think you now have the chance to make a shitload of money."

"How?" I asked. For money usually tends to give me a very wide berth.

He said that my virile organ had proven itself to be an excellent defense against a possible bear attack—far more economically sized than a firearm and presumably less toxic than bear spray. All I needed to do now was find someone to manufacture replicas of it, and I would be set for life.

A confession: I haven't yet followed up on David's suggestion for how I might dramatically improve my finances.

⌐⌐⌐⌐

SEAL HUNTING

One summer afternoon near Saqqaq, West Greenland, I was seated in a small boat with a local who suddenly raised his rifle and shot at a seal, missing it. He did so on purpose. He shot at it again and missed it on purpose again.

The reason for his lousy aim? He wanted to wear out the seal so that when our boat came close to it, he could harpoon it. If he succeeded in killing it with his gun, the seal would sink before he reached it. At a colder time of year, he would shoot to kill, since the seal's extra blubber would keep it afloat.

When the seal seemed worn out, the hunter paddled over to it, raised his *unaaq* (wooden harpoon), and whacked it hard. The blood from its head and whiskered face trailed scarlet in the water.

The seal did not seem to appreciate this unpleasant act, and it struggled far longer than I would have expected. The hunter now forced his harpoon deeper into the seal. The animal swerved back and forth energetically, doubtless registering its pain as well as trying to dislodge the harpoon. Meanwhile, the orange float attached to the harpoon swerved just as energetically as the seal.

"Now I will kill her," the hunter said.

"Her?" I asked.

"This is a lady seal. You can see she's going to have a baby. That's why she's fighting so hard."

The Greenlander raised his rifle, then gave the seal a hard knock on the head with its stock, and she stopped fighting. He and I began dragging the dead seal into the boat. Our hands and anoraks ended up covered with the seal's blood.

"She is good lady," he told me, "for she will make my family very happy when they eat her . . ."

⌐⌐⌐

AVIAN INTELLECT

The Vuntut Gwich'in village of Old Crow in the Yukon Territory is not to be confused with the bourbon whiskey that goes by the same name. But the village's name could just as readily be Old Raven, since ravens in northern Canada are commonly called crows.

During a visit to the village, I noticed ravens everywhere—on power poles, on the roofs of houses, and sitting at the top of the cross on the church's steeple, as if this were *their* community. I even saw several ravens hanging upside down on a power line, then somersaulting over, and then hanging upside down again. This was doubtless their playground.

At one point a Gwich'in man took me to his extensive backyard, where one of his sled dogs, an Alaska malamute, was tethered to a post. "Watch this," he told me.

He gave the dog a fish dinner. It wasn't long before two ravens swooped down, one alighting on the dog's back and the other landing right next to the fish. The dog kept turning its white muzzle and trying to bite the raven hopping about on its back, but to no avail.

Meanwhile, the other raven dined on approximately half the fish.

Now the ravens traded places. The well-fed one hopped onto the dog's back, provoking more failed bites, while the other scarfed down the other half of the dog's fish dinner.

At last the ravens flew off, flashing their black iridescent plumage against the sunlight-spangled sky. One of them turned its head toward the dog and uttered a series of gurgling croaks that perhaps meant something like this: "What a pity you allowed yourself to be domesticated, dear chap."

⌐⌐⌐⌐

MEETING WITH A MUSK OX

Diana Island is an obscure speck of land in Hudson Strait inhabited by musk oxen rather than by humans. Wandering around the island, I saw quite a few clumps of musk ox underfur snagged by the serrated edges of dwarf birch leaves. Known as qiviut, this underfur is a thick mass of fibers perhaps eight times warmer than lamb's wool. I own a qiviut cap, and when I'm wearing it, I'm so warm that I feel like throwing off all my clothes and frisking about in the nude . . . even if the temperature is below zero.

I decided I needed an equally warm scarf. As I squatted down to pull some qiviut from a ground-hugging birch, I heard a series of rough snorts and looked up to see a large musk ox standing less than fifty feet away from me. The expression on its bearded face (the Inuit call a muskox *umingmaq*, "The Bearded One") seemed to say, "Get out of my territory, dude." The bony plate between its horns gave its head the appearance of armor.

The musk ox now lowered that head and charged. Consider a Jeep Cherokee with a pair of very nasty hood ornaments bearing down on you, and you'll get a reasonably good idea of what it's like to be charged by a musk ox. Except a Jeep Cherokee is a contemporary vehicle, where this woolly ungulate is an Ice Age survivor.

For a moment, I was so stunned by the oncoming animal that I froze. Then I turned and ran. Actually, I turned, tripped, and plunged headlong onto an outcropping of granite. When I looked up, the musk ox was grazing on some sedge and seemed completely indifferent to me.

My only injury was a painful imprint of the Canadian Shield on my left cheek, a souvenir from my visit to Diana Island that I had with me for several months. Unlike most souvenirs, it was received cash-free.

ⅎⅎⅎⅎ

THE INUIT *PUJOALUK*

If you mention mushrooms to most Inuit, you'll probably get an expression of disgust. For they consider mushrooms the *anaq* (shit) of shooting stars. Why such a seemingly unusual belief? Because a shooting star hurtles across the late summer sky, trailing languid flares of detritus behind it. The following morning mushrooms appear on the tundra . . . flagrantly inedible mushrooms, for who would want to eat the fecal matter of a shooting star?

Yet there's a fungal entity called a *pujoaluk* that the Inuit eagerly collect, although they do so for medicinal rather than culinary purposes. Elizabeth Nukarratiq, an Inuit elder from Kimmirut on Baffin Island, told me about this type of medicinal.

"In the late summer and fall, we gather all the *pujoaluit* we can find," she said. "They have a dry powder in them that stops bleeding and heals a wound. This is much better than having an *angakok* (shaman) lick the wound, which was done a lot in the old days."

From a caribou hide tote bag, she removed some *pujoaluit*, which turned out to be several *Lycoperdon* puffball species.

If you jab your hand with a knife or cut your leg with a saw blade, you sprinkle the spores from one of these puffballs onto the wound, and those spores will stop the flow of blood, she remarked. She added that a still solid *pujoaluk*—one whose interior has not yet turned to spores—won't have any effect at all on a wound.

It's not surprising that this practice works, for chitosan, a component of fungal cell walls, bonds with a person's red blood cells, forming a red gel-like clot that serves as a styptic. Also, those spores possess strong antibiotic properties (note: a far better word than antibiotic is "antibacterial"), which help with the wound's healing—as long as that wound is somewhat modest. For a deep wound, it's best to see a doctor.

I told her that *pujoaluit* were commonly eaten where I came from, but they were never applied to wounds. She looked baffled. Another example of the curious habits of White People, her expression seemed to say.

Since I didn't suffer from any sort of wound during my visit to Baffin Island, I didn't have the opportunity to put the immune-activating properties of a *pujoaluk* to the test. Well, I did end up with sort of a wound: I scratched one of my myriad mosquito bites so aggressively that it bled. Not having a puffball handy, I put a boring bandage on the bleeding bite.

ᒐᒐᒐᒐ

STARVATION CUISINE

With his sagging jowls, bald pate, and general portliness, not to mention his habit of constantly toting a Bible, Sir John Franklin (1786–1847) resembled a retired English vicar rather than an Arctic explorer. Truth to tell, his competence as an Arctic explorer was not much better than a typical English vicar's would be. Toward the end of his life, he was known as "the man who ate his boots." He could just as readily have been known as "the man who ate lichens."

In 1819, Franklin led an overland expedition from Hudson Bay to the northwestern part of the Canadian Arctic. Called the Coppermine expedition, its purpose was multifold: to make meteorological observations, to determine the coordinates of Canada's northern coast, and to learn something about the local indigenous people.

The return journey from the Arctic coast occurred during the late fall and winter. Franklin and his men had run out of food and, to allay the threat of starvation, they ate tripe-de-roche or rock tripe. This name refers to several different *Umbilicaria* lichen species that look like slices of a cow's stomach affixed to a granitic rock.

Here are some references to this lichen from *Franklin's Narrative of a Journey to the Shores of the Polar Sea*: "The wont of *tripe de roche* caused us to go supperless to bed." "In the evening, there being no *tripe de roche,* we were compelled to satisfy the cravings of hunger by eating a gun cover." "The *tripe de roche* had hitherto afforded us our chief support, and we naturally felt a great uneasiness at being deprived of it."

The support provided by the lichen would have consisted primarily of carbohydrates, which are one of the human body's main sources of energy. A piece of tripe-de-roche contains 10 to 15 percent more carbs than an equivalent portion of, say, a potato. It also contains more than the equivalent portion of a gun cover . . .

Canadian First Nations people commonly ate tripe-de-roche. The Northern Cree used it (and still use it) to thicken their fish broths, and the Labrador Innu ate it when there was no other food available, referring to it as *windigo wakaw* (cannibal's cabbage).

It's been suggested that George Washington and his soldiers may have survived their difficult overwintering at Valley Forge by eating tripe-de-roche. If this is in fact true, then the United States owes its freedom from British tyranny to a foliose lichen.

All of the aforementioned diners boiled their tripe-de-roche before eating it. Either Franklin's men were too weak and weary to boil the lichen, or—more likely—they weren't aware that the lichen's complex carbohydrates and high acid content make it difficult to digest when eaten raw. Thus it's not surprising that most members of the expedition suffered from what Franklin called "bowel complaints" as a result of eating the lichen.

By the end, half of the expedition's twenty-two men had died. Maybe Franklin himself would have died if he hadn't eaten tripe-de-roche. But if he had died, he wouldn't have been able to disappear twenty-five years later during his ill-fated Northwest Passage expedition. That disappearance inspired perhaps the largest manhunt in human history, and although Franklin's body wasn't found, the manhunters did succeed in mapping a large part of the Canadian Arctic. You could say that this mapping, perhaps like the birth of the United States, also owes its existence to a foliose lichen.

Now let's travel forward to April 2019. At a Franklin conference hosted by the Mystic Seaport Museum in Mystic, Connecticut, I served boiled tripe-de-roche (specifically, *Umbilicaria mammulata*) to the Franklin experts in attendance. Most of them sampled it for scholarly reasons, but they were not particularly delighted by either its texture or its flavor, not even when they daubed it in the Angostura bitters or fish sauce that I brought.

Of course, none of these Franklin experts was even close to starvation.

ᴧᴧᴧᴧ

AN INUIT DELICACY

Once upon a time, in Igloolik, Nunavut, a local Inuk named Simon offered me a culinary item that met my gaze with a seemingly unhappy gaze of its own.

"Eye of seal," Simon observed. "Very good. Tastes like raw egg."

"Do you ever cook it?" I asked.

"Inuit people don't like it cooked. Much better this way." Whereupon he began squeezing the soft and greasy eye into his mouth as if it were a large grape.

I quickly looked away. As perhaps my host himself would have done if I had taken a bite of broccoli, asparagus, or cauliflower.

My host now offered me another seal eye. In the past, I'd happily eaten Inuit foods like raw *tugtup kumait* (warble fly larvae), half-cooked *nirukkaq* (the stomach contents of a musk ox in winter), and *igunaq* (rotten walrus meat). But this was different, since eyes—especially raw eyes—are different from other parts of the body. And especially a raw eye affixed to a large clump of optic nerves.

Simon was watching me in such a way that I figured I would be demeaning his culture if I didn't eat the seal eye. But as I raised the eye tentatively to my mouth, I looked at it, and it seemed to be saying, *please don't eat me, dear sir.* It resembled a cute little puppy's eye.

All at once there was a knock on the door. A postman had arrived with a package. In Simon's absence, I quickly stashed the seal eye in my backpack. When he returned, I said, "That *isi* [seal eye] was damn good," and rubbed my stomach. Simon gave me a happy smile.

Later, when I removed my camera and notebook from my rucksack, I found them covered with the somewhat gloopy material that came from the seal eye I'd deposited there. I was a bit annoyed, of course. But I was also roused enough to write this short essay.

ᴜᴜᴜᴜ

DOG FOOD

On a visit to Greenland's capital Nuuk, I went to an open-air market called Braedtet (the Plank) in search of my supper. Displayed on tables as well as piled on the ground, I saw dead kittiwakes, briskets of reindeer, walrus aortas, dried whale meat, *mikiaq* (decomposing seal heads), and various types of fish, along with head-shot seals skinned to the nose and hung vertically on ropes.

Needless to say, there were no carrots, cauliflower, asparagus, or brussels sprouts. Nor were there any beans, which Greenlanders call *niliguaq*, "a thing that makes you fart."

Soon a short woman with shoulders like a fullback's tried to interest me in buying some *qimmeq* (dog). She pointed to some light brown meat lying in a heap on a table.

"*Qimmiaraq* [puppy]?" I asked. For I knew that the puppies of sled dogs were occasionally strangled and their fur used to provide trim for a child's parka. Might a dead puppy sans fur be considered cuisine?

The woman shook her head, uttering a word I didn't catch—probably the local word for an adult dog that had outlived its usefulness as a sled animal, and whose sole purpose now was to be useful as food. (Note: As the custom of using sled dogs has declined in Greenland, so has the custom of eating them.)

Unlike explorer Vilhjalmur Stefansson, who balked at the idea of eating man's best friend, I had no qualms about doing so myself. On the one hand, I have much better friends than *Canis familiaris*. On the other hand, I was curious about the taste of a former sled dog. So I asked for a pound or so of the meat. After the woman took my kroner, she handed the meat to me, saying, "*Nerilluarisi!*" (Bon appétit!)

Back at my tent I cut the meat into chunks and cooked those chunks for a relatively long time over my Primus stove. Since I didn't have any basil, dill, oregano, garlic, or thyme with my gear, I was obliged to eat the meat without a seasoning. But this at least gave me a good idea of how Greenlandic sled dog actually tastes.

How, in fact, did the meat taste? For starters, it was so chewy that I felt like I was eating mostly muscle and sinew, which isn't surprising for a lifelong puller of sleds. It also had a generic gamy flavor. Even though the dog's primary food would have been fish, the meat did not have a fishy flavor at all. If I wanted to be off-putting, I'd say that it tasted like a wet dog smells. A kinder way to describe it would be to say that it would have bene-fited from some hot sauce or perhaps vinegar.

Here's perhaps a still kinder way to describe it: by dining on a Greenlandic sled dog, I was again putting to work an animal that had devoted its life to working for my species.

⌐⌐⌐⌐

A DISH OF DEFECATION

If you tell a Greenlander to "eat shit," it's not really an insult. That's because ptarmigan droppings are considered, if not exactly haute cuisine, at least a decent edible in certain parts of Greenland. These droppings are collected in the winter when they're dry rather than at other times of the year when they're unpleasantly gooey.

Sometimes called snow chickens, ptarmigans have feathered earflaps, eyelids, and nostrils, so they have no problem surviving frigid winters. Even during such winters, a ptarmigan will remain stationary for long periods and, in doing so, it may defecate fifty or more pellets in a single place. Thus the fecal forager doesn't have to search far and wide for his or her food.

Explorer-raconteur Peter Freuchen wrote that ptarmigan droppings tasted not unlike Roquefort cheese. As for myself, I ate them cooked in rancid seal oil twice in Greenland, and on both occasions, the flavor of the droppings was camouflaged by the seal oil. Roquefort, maybe; but seal oil, yes. I wanted to eat them without a camouflage, and so on a winter trip to Iceland, I collected a batch I found near the Stefansson Arctic Institute in Akureyri, Iceland.

Here I should mention that the droppings in question came from a willow ptarmigan (*Lagopus lagopus*), while the droppings I'd had in Greenland were from a rock ptarmigan (*Lagopus muta*). Even so, the diet of the two different species was similar, which meant the taste of the droppings would probably be similar, too.

In Hjalteyri, a small village near Akureyri, my friend Lene and I prepared the Icelandic version of the previously described Greenlandic recipe. In lieu of seal oil, we used sheep fat. *Non-rancid* sheep fat, I should add.

After Lene emptied the bag of droppings into a cooking pot, I offered a prayer to Sterculius, the Roman god of excrement, to bless our dish. As a further blessing, I sprinkled some turmeric into the pot.

While we cooked the droppings on top of an outdoor stove, we deliberated on the best libation to accompany it. At last we decided on Birkir, an Icelandic schnapps flavored with a birch twig. This drink seemed to us highly appropriate, since birch catkins constitute a part of the winter diet of ptarmigan (another part is willow buds).

After fifteen or so minutes, we removed the pot from the stove and settled down on a bench to dine on *Merde de lagopede a l'islande*. I impaled three or four droppings on my fork and lifted them to my mouth.

The texture of what I chewed was crunchy, while the flavor suggested some sort of plant or vegetable—doubtless the catkins or buds of the original diner subjected to fermentation from the ptarmigan's stomach fluids.

Lene and I evaluated this flavor, and with proverbial shit-eating grins on our faces, gave it a solid B rating. It tasted more like slightly tangy Velveeta than Roquefort cheese, however.

At one point a local fisherman wandered by and asked what we happened to be eating. "*Rjupa skitur!*" Lene laughed, then emulated the cackle of a ptarmigan by chortling "*kek-kek-kek.*"

Hákarl (rotten shark's meat) is Iceland's national dish, with *svið* (singed sheep's head) ranking a close second, so you probably won't be surprised to hear that the fisherman didn't bat an eyelid. Indeed, he requested a sample. After he had taken a few bites, he said, "Not bad, but it needs some salt . . ."

While the droppings of a ptarmigan may not be everyone's idea of a culinary treat, I would choose it any day of the week over whatever McDonald's puts between its buns.

ⴀⴀⴀⴀ

IN AN ICELANDIC FOREST

I was walking through Iceland's oldest forest in Hallormsstaður with Þröstur Eysteinsson, director of the Icelandic Forest Service. Most of the trees in this unusually dense forest were downy birches (*Betula pubescens*), the world's northernmost broad-leaved tree. At a height of fifty or so feet, the downy birch is a veritable dwarf compared to a redwood or a Douglas fir, but at least it gives the lie to the popular joke that asks this question: What do you do if you get lost in an Icelandic forest? The answer is, of course, you stand up.

The trees around us were a hundred years old, but they were so gnarly, withered, and pockmarked that they looked like they were a thousand years old. Such antiquated features are typical of downy birches, even young ones. Their down is a coating of hairs that act like a parka, protecting the trees in cold weather. If the trees had been straight, firm, and tidy-looking, something would have been wrong with them. In fact, they might have been dying or even dead.

When we ended up in a part of the forest alongside the well-traveled ring road, Þröstur recited the well-known poem "Hríslan og lækurinn" ("The Birch Tree and the Stream") by nineteenth-century poet Páll Ólafsson. In this work, the poet envisions himself as a stream into which a nearby birch tree is dropping its leaves in the fall and, by doing so, caressing him with them. Thröstur pointed to a particularly gnarly birch tree. This is the same tree that was caressing the poet 150 years ago, he said.

Hardly more than a dozen feet away, tour buses were roaring by, their occupants oblivious to Iceland's most celebrated tree.

⌐⌐⌐⌐

STARING SESSION

With an Inuk, I was exploring an eastern part of Foxe Basin in Nunavut. In the distance, off to our motorboat's starboard, was the ghostly outline of drifting ice floes. As we got closer, I saw a relatively large floe on which a dozen or so paunchy walruses huddled together in an attitude of repose. The air was misty with their breaths. Their downcurved tusks gleamed brilliantly in the sunlight, and as the boat got still closer, I began to see their spiky whiskers and Colonel Blimp jowls.

"*Aivik*," my Inuit guide said, using the Inuktitut word for walrus. "We eat it all the time. We even eat the clams in its stomach!"

I now asked him an R-rated question. "Does the *oosik* have a purpose for your people?" Note: An *oosik* is the long, perpetually hard baculum (penis bone) of a walrus.

"*Aap!*" he said. "A boy who kills his first *aivik*, he keeps the *oosik* because it will bring him good luck in the years to come." His grin gave more than a hint of what he meant by "good luck."

When we got several feet closer, my guide cut the motor. He didn't want to disturb the walrus, he said.

For a disturbed walrus is an aggressive walrus, and an aggressive walrus might try to defend itself and its territory by attacking our boat.

"Have you ever been attacked by an *aivik*?" I asked.

"*Aaggaqai* [not yet], but my father was attacked by one. It propped its tusks onto his boat and looked at him angrily. '*Unataa takugit*,' he shouted at it. That means 'You lookin' for a fight?'" He slapped the animal's face with his paddle, and it grunted and slid back into the water.

But these particular walrus weren't at all aggressive. Quite the contrary. Once they became aware of our presence, they waddled off to the edge of the floe and dove into the sea. A while later their tusked heads surfaced as a group, bobbed for a minute or two, disappeared, and then resurfaced, regarding us with at best a mild curiosity.

But a single old bull with two-foot-long tusks and five or more inches of blubber stood his ground on the ice floe, giving me such a long hard stare with its bloodshot eyes. I stared right back, for I happen to enjoy staring sessions with animals far more so than I enjoy staring sessions with my fellow human beings. After a while, the bull softened its stare and began gazing at me as if I were a kindred spirit. He was close enough that I could smell his breath, which had the aroma of the clams he'd been eating.

This staring session occurred almost twenty-five years ago. If I returned to the same locale today, I probably wouldn't see any walrus. After all, climate change would have melted a large percentage of the ice floes on which they sit and stare, not to mention mate and give birth.

⎍⎍⎍

THE ORIGIN OF BLOODTHIRSTINESS

Outside the town of Qaqortoq, West Greenland, a local Inuk named Jorge and I were being mobbed by mosquitoes. I quickly reached into my rucksack, grabbed a tube of bug dope, and smeared it all over my face and neck, only to realize I'd grabbed a tube of latex glue. By doing this, I confirmed nineteenth-century Arctic explorer Elisha Kent Kane's statement that "prudence and foolhardiness lie within sight of each other up here."

At the sight of my face, Jorge burst into riotous laughter. "You look just like a hundred-year-old elder," he said as I was trying to scrape the glue off my face with my nails. After he stopped laughing, he said, "Let me tell you a story about mosquitoes . . ."

He began:

Once upon a time all the mosquitoes in the world lived on a small island in Igaliku Fjord. They kept entirely to themselves, never leaving the island, just paddling their little kayaks around it.

On the mainland, there lived a man named Niliq who was always robbing people. The last straw came when Niliq stole a boat full of whale meat. He rowed that boat over to the mosquito island, where he thought no one would find him. But his victims followed the smell of the whale meat to the island and, finding Niliq there, decided to punish him for his thievery. They beat him to a pulp with their clubs and left him lying on the rocks.

The mosquitoes had been going through a period of very bad hunting. They looked down on Niliq and thought he might ease their hunger. So, they started to drink his blood. What a nice taste! they thought. They drank more and more of it, until Niliq was drained of his blood.

After that, the mosquitoes left their island and started hunting people, since now that they had tasted our blood, they preferred it to any other food.

"Now you know why mosquitoes like to suck our blood," Jorge told me. "It's because we're so *blodtorstig* [bloodthirsty] ourselves."

By this time, I had removed almost all of the glue from my face, and mosquitoes were once again landing on it, piercing my skin, and becoming gravid with my blood. In other words, they were exhibiting the behavior they'd acquired from my own bloodthirsty species.

⌐⌐⌐

ORNITHOLOGY IN THE YUKON

On a visit to the Yukon, a birder friend drove me to the Son of War Eagle landfill a few miles outside the town of Whitehorse. "Last year I saw two uncommon species for the Yukon here—a Brewer's blackbird and an American pipit," he told me.

Shortly after we arrived, we saw a raven perched magisterially on top of a huge pyramid of tires. Wiggling its wedge-shaped tail, the bird peered down as if it were the monarch of all it surveyed. On the mounds of garbage directly beneath the pyramid, there were other ravens, one trying to scarf down a bagel, another with what looked like a dog biscuit in its beak, and yet another thrusting its head hopefully into a black plastic bag, and still another eating little chunks of a ragged mountain goat hide.

For a scavenger like a raven, a place like this is an absolute delight. Indeed, more than a thousand ravens had spent the previous winter there. According to my friend, they did the equivalent of dumpster diving to keep warm—periodically burying their bodies in the compost. For warm compost is more effective than the specialized feathers on a raven's nostrils for warding off the Yukon's subzero winter temperatures.

Soon we were seeing magpies, Canada jays, Thayer's gulls, herring gulls, lesser black-backed gulls, ospreys, pine grosbeaks, and a few dowitchers all perched on, pecking at, or waddling around a veritable smorgasbord of such human throwaways as fish bones, chicken carcasses, pizza crusts, and moldy bread.

To survive, most northern birds need to eat more than half their weight in food on a daily basis. This is not a problem for even the heftiest bird at the Son of War Eagle landfill.

There were also quite a few bald eagles. Despite their heroic reputation, they seemed perfectly at home with the garbage. And why not? They were getting a far more varied diet than they'd get during a salmon run.

Some of the eagles seemed wary of me, but others appeared to be waiting eagerly for a handout. One eagle approached me and, in doing so, knocked aside a raven. This brusque gesture reminded me of Benjamin Franklin's remark that eagles are birds "of a bad moral character."

But not all eagles are rude to ravens. The landfill's attendant told me he'd seen an eagle and a raven who were, in his words, "buddies."

I asked him if that meant they had a love relationship. "You could say that, yes," he replied.

Increasingly, the eagles—like the ravens—were spending their winters here. The Yukon Bird Club's Christmas Bird Count in 2006 listed only one eagle, but in 2010 there were fifteen, and now there are many more.

Natural selection among birds can happen fast, very fast, especially when both food and nesting sites are readily available. With all the discarded bed frames, rotting plywood, and old tires, the nesting sites here were myriad. Indeed, almost everything on the premises can be considered a ready-made nest—no cavity pecking and no collecting of twigs, grass, or leaves necessary.

As we were leaving, the attendant mentioned that a California condor had visited the landfill several years ago. A California condor—remarkable! Later I learned that the bird in question had been a turkey vulture. But given a turkey vulture's usual geographical range, the fact that one showed up at the Son of War Eagle landfill was only slightly less unusual than if a California condor had swooped down and carried off the remnant of a pepperoni pizza.

I had an uncomfortable vision of the not too distant future, a time when the majority of creatures both great and small would be relying on us humans for both their room and board. At such a time, I can easily imagine a raven, upon being asked whether it wanted to return to the wild, croaking "Nevermore."

ᒐᒥ

STICK FIGURES

For several days, a cold drizzle oozed down from the hoary sky, keeping me in my tent on Nunavik's Ungava Peninsula. I got so accustomed to my Primus stove's hiss that when I stepped out of my tent to answer nature's call, I wondered why the outside world wasn't hissing, too.

At last the drizzle stopped, the dark gray clouds scurried away, and I took a hike on the adjacent tundra. Everywhere I looked, I saw a landscape blanketed green with arctic heather (*Cassiope tetragona*) and punctuated with red and yellow flowers, along with the fluffy white pompoms of arctic cotton (*Eriophorum callitrix*). One area was almost totally blue with a flowering of arctic harebells (*Campanula uniflora*).

There were also hordes of mosquitoes. Each swat of my hand on my forehead dispatched perhaps half a dozen of them. While I was engaged in this swatting, a stick figure approached me. Was it my imagination, or did the look on the figure's face say, "Please help me"?

This wasn't the first such figure I'd seen in these parts. Nor would it be the last. Here's the reason for its emaciated condition:

In the Arctic, caribou cows used to calf when there was snow on the ground. Now that the snow melts before their calving season in June, pools of meltwater are ready for egg-laying mosquitoes well before the cows give birth . . . and when they do give birth, literal clouds of mosquitoes eagerly go after them. The cows end up paying almost no attention to their newborn calves because they're either scratching themselves in the underbrush or desperately trying to keep themselves from being exsanguinated—drained of their blood.

Let me add that, if given the choice, a mosquito would rather go after a caribou than a human-type being. For isoleucine, an amino acid necessary for a mosquito's egg production, is deficient in humans but dramatically present in cervids like caribou, elk, and moose.

Assuming that the caribou calves survive the loss of their own isoleucine, they usually tend to wander off by themselves. They have no idea what foods they should eat or where to find those foods, since only their mothers could provide them with tutorials on (for example) *Cladonia* lichens, one of their primary foods. Thus they get thinner and thinner, until they become hardly more than bags of bones.

As I gazed at the stick figure gazing at me, I felt responsible for its condition. After all, the machinations of my species had instigated the premature melting of the snow. Was there anything I could do to remedy the poor creature's condition? I asked myself. I could think of only one answer, and that was to take it out of its misery. But when I picked up a rock and advanced toward the calf, it quickly wobbled away from me in search of another would-be mother.

ⁿⁿⁿⁿ

Encounters
with
Remote Places

A LOST KNIFE

Ecologist Aldo Leopold defined wilderness as "an area that possesses no possibility of conveyance by mechanical means."

Welcome to Mansel Island in Canada's eastern Hudson Bay, where there are no cars, tundra buggies, ATVs, SUVs, motorcycles, or airplanes, all of which are mechanical conveyances. As my Inuit guide Jake and I explored this giant uninhabited chunk of limestone, I was obliged to use the very best conveyance of all—my feet.

It was a raw, gray day with drizzle and a leaden rack of clouds. At one point we discovered an old Inuit burial cairn on a hillock. The cairn had a hole on top, so I peered inside and saw a well-preserved skeleton curled into a fetal position. This suggested that the inhabitant of the cairn had lived in the late Thule Period (maybe four hundred years ago) because Inuit from that era believed their dead should exit the world in precisely the same posture as they entered it.

I now performed what might be called an illicit act. Sticking my pocket knife into the cairn, I gently turned the bleached skull so it was facing me. The condition of the teeth would tell me whether it belonged to a male or female. If it belonged to a woman, the teeth would be worn down from chewing skins, but if it belonged to a man, the teeth would hardly be worn at all. As it happened, the skull turned out to be a man's.

"I don't think you should have done that," Jake said. "That guy could be an *angakok* [shaman], and he might decide to take revenge on you—maybe stick a knife in *your* skull."

"I'll take my chances," I replied.

Later, when we were a few hundred yards from the cairn, I reached for my knife, but it wasn't in its case. I looked into my pockets, but I still couldn't locate it. I investigated the outer shell of my rucksack, a mesh of flaps and pockets, but it wasn't there, either. I asked myself if I would soon become insensible. For there's an old saying in the Canadian outback that "a knifeless man is a lifeless man."

"Maybe you left it at the cairn," Jake said. We walked back to the cairn, and I looked all around, but I still couldn't seem to find it.

All at once I saw an arctic fox standing next to the cairn and gazing at me with what looked like a wry grin.

This seemed somewhat odd, since arctic foxes are seldom this fearless with respect to my species, especially so in the North, where they're commonly trapped for their fur.

Occasionally, a fox will engage in high-pitched barking when it sees a person, then beat a hasty retreat; once in a while it'll retreat only a short distance, then peer quizzically at that person behind a boulder. But this one uttered not a sound, nor did it retreat at all.

With the fox standing fearlessly only ten or so feet away from us, Jake proclaimed: "That proves it. The person in the grave, he *is* an *angakok*, and he's taken on the form of a *akunnatuq* [fox]. He's telling you, 'I've stolen your knife so you'll never touch my skull with it again.'"

However much I looked, I still couldn't locate the knife, so I had no choice but to conclude that the shamanic fox had indeed stolen it.

⌐⌐⌐⌐

A WALK ON THE WILD SIDE

"I don't even know what street Canada is on," Al Capone reputedly declared. Even if he did know what street Canada was on, the celebrated gangster wouldn't have known what street Rigolet, Labrador, is on. For Rigolet, a small (pop. three hundred), mostly Inuit village, is not on any street. You can get there only by hopping a plane or taking a ferry.

Given Rigolet's isolation as well as its small population, it's one of the last places in the world where you'd expect to find a boardwalk longer than the one in Atlantic City. Having arrived in Rigolet, I met the mayor, Jack Shiwak, and he told me about the origin of this boardwalk.

"We missed the boardwalk that once connected the old Hudson's Bay Company buildings here, so we decided to build a new one . . . a very long new one." he said. "Of course, the Atlantic City boardwalk was always in the backs of our minds."

"But you don't seem to have any gambling casinos here," I joked.

"True, but we do have a fascinating archaeological site," Jack replied.

I decided not to walk the boardwalk's entire six miles, ending in that archaeological site, all at once. There were too many opportunities to stand and stare at wooden crosses that were tilted at every angle of the compass, seals whose bobbing heads punctuated the nearby sea, and the occasional moose contentedly nibbling on leaves, bark, and twigs.

On one side of the boardwalk was boreal forest, and on the other were the tranquil waters of Hamilton Inlet. As I walked, the only sound that didn't come from the natural world was the sound of my own feet on wood. The natural sounds included the *chuf-chufs* of Canada jays, the flutelike calls of pine grosbeaks, the skittering of arctic hares across the boardwalk, and the raucous laughter of gulls, which seemed to suggest that I was an utterly hilarious creature because I was walking rather than flying.

Occasionally, I would leave the boardwalk and wander into a dark spruce forest sprinkled with white-limbed poplars and a few birch trees. On one of these occasions, I was answering nature's proverbial call when I saw a black bear rummaging for berries. The bear looked at me, then quickly looked away. What a well-mannered creature, I thought.

Walking on the boardwalk, I often saw minke whales rising and spouting, but I seldom saw any boats in Hamilton Inlet. After all, the water contained large amounts of methyl mercury due to the damming of upstream rivers. Traveling up the food chain, this neurotoxin is a bio-accumulator that makes the eating of seals, fish, and birds a very risky proposition. As a result, hunting in Rigolet is mostly done in the local market.

One day I met a local nurse of advanced years who told me she walked to the end of the boardwalk and back almost every day, a distance of twelve miles. When I indicated I hadn't made it to the end yet, she looked at me as if I were a total wimp.

At last I did reach the end, where the remains of three eighteenth-century Inuit sod houses lie directly above a Paleo-Eskimo site several thousand years old. From these sod houses, curious artifacts have been excavated—for example, an Ottoman pipe. I imagined an eighteenth-century Inuk smoking this exotic pipe and gazing contentedly at minke whales rising and spouting in Hamilton Inlet.

On my last day, I was walking back to Rigolet from the archaeological site when I happened to see a figure emerging from the dense fog. That figure turned out to be one of the few tourists I'd encountered on the boardwalk.

"I've heard this is longer than Atlantic City's, eh?" the fellow said, instantly identifying himself as a Canadian.

"I don't even know what street Atlantic City is on," I replied.

ꟷꟷꟷ

ANOTHER WALK ON THE WILD SIDE

"You won't see any souls on the island except for little auks and puffins," observed the Icelandic fisherman who dropped me off at Krossbukta Bay on the west coast of Jan Mayen.

The fellow was more or less correct. As I began wandering north along a seemingly endless beach, I didn't encounter a single beachgoer. This isn't surprising, since Jan Mayen is a Norway-owned island far to the north of Iceland, far to the east of Greenland, at the tip of the North Atlantic Ridge, and thus decidedly remote. Its only human inhabitants are a handful of Norwegians who occupy a weather station on the other side of the 146-square-mile island.

Right away I saw drift logs from Siberian rivers scattered all over the beach. Transported around the High Arctic by the clockwise Beaufort Gyre as well as the Transpolar Drift, they'd been shuttled south to these parts by the strong East Greenland Current. The journey from Siberia to Jan Mayen might have taken as long as a hundred years, but the logs didn't seem to mind, for they looked perfectly fit.

I alternately circumnavigated and hopped over these myriad drift logs as I headed in the direction of Atlantic City. *Atlantic City?* Was I going to venture all the way to New Jersey? Stay tuned . . .

In addition to little auks and puffins, the twisted black lava cliffs adjacent to the beach hosted a large population of fulmars, kittiwakes, glaucous gulls, and black guillemots. Living birds nested in these cliffs, and a remarkable number of dead bird bodies lay in rest on the beach itself. Their frail cages were flexed at grotesque angles, and many of their bleached beaks were wide open, as if they wanted to breathe the island's pristine arctic air even in death. The mingling of these avian corpses with drift logs lying askew, isolated, or piled high made me feel like I was wandering around inside a work of surrealist art.

At one point I saw an eider duck seated contentedly on her nest, with her brownish-gray down giving her eggs an exceptional degree of warmth. I approached her, and she gazed at me with virtually no interest, as if her eggs were what mattered to her, not a certain meddle-some hominid. "Sorry to bother you, dear," I said, as I slowly backed away.

At another point I saw a stone epitaph atop a ridge. Might this be a memorial to a sailor or explorer shipwrecked on these unsettled shores? Or maybe a memorial to a deceased inhabitant of Atlantic City? I had no way of knowing, since the name and dates on the stone were camouflaged by a greenish-yellow crustose lichen. No matter. Lichens are the dominant life form in the Arctic, so it seemed appropriate that data on a gray rock should be replaced by a lichen.

In the distance, I could see the 7,470-foot strata volcano Beerenberg, which rises from the sea at 71 N and is the world's northernmost active volcano. Witnessing Beerenberg from his curragh-like boat, the Irish monk Saint Brendan the Navigator thought its giant ash plumes indicated a throng of hyperactive blacksmiths laboring away on the summit. Myself, I thought these plumes were gesturing me not to go any farther, lest I end up blanketed by volcanic ash.

This last speculation inspired me to look at my watch. I'd been walking for five hours, and it was time for me to head back to where the fisherman had dropped me off, since he said he'd pick me up in eight hours.

As it happened, I wasn't really concerned that I hadn't made it to Jan Mayen's Atlantic City, which wouldn't have been a casino-riddled, boardwalk-girdled place. Rather, it was a whimsically named American radio and weather station from the Second World War that now consisted of only a few ruined barracks and a ruined sauna. It might have been an interesting destination, probably more so than New Jersey's Atlantic City, but it's the journey not the destination that matters.

So, it was that I hopped over drift logs and dead birds as I happily made my way back along the black lava sand to Krossbukta Bay.

ᒡᒪᒡᒪ

MAKING CONTACT

During the 1980s, I made several visits to Angmagssalik (now Tasiilaq), East Greenland, to collect ethnographic lore from the locals. At one point I asked a hunter if he'd ever encountered any Erqigdlit, a race of doglike people who reputedly lived on or near the Greenland ice cap. Might they be dying out now that the ice cap was melting? I wondered.

The man said he'd never met any Erqigdlit, but he had once gone hunting on a fjord just north of Skjoldungen and found a recently abandoned campsite that had tent rings, discarded skins, and a rock that seemed to be shaped for flensing. This, to him, indicated a group of people still living like their ancestors.

Another local said he'd been to the same place and found a map carved from driftwood that looked exactly like the maps his people carved before the arrival of Europeans.

Why do you think that it was a map and not simply a much-damaged piece of driftwood? I asked him.

"Because it showed an exact outline of the fjord where I found it," he said.

Suddenly a lightbulb went on in my mind. An uncontacted group of people living on a remote fjord in southeast Greenland! I decided I would travel down there and try to locate them myself. In the brightness of that same lightbulb, I had an image of a rough-hewn hunter-gatherer staring at me, a visitor from a different era, as if I came from outer space.

I mentioned the prospect of uncontacted Greenlanders to a Danish friend in Angmagssalik. He was no less excited than I. He said the two of us could travel down to the fjords north of Skjoldungen in his motorized fishing boat and search for what he called "these Stone Agers." The media, he added, would be really excited if we found them.

Upon hearing the word "media," I began to have my doubts. These doubts increased when I found myself talking again with the man who'd told me about the driftwood map. "Those unknown people, you must leave them alone," he said. "Let them live or starve, as they choose. *Attuniannaguk!* Please don't touch them!"

I now found myself with cold feet. Not the sort of cold feet that a person with the wrong footwear might get in these parts, but a feeling that it wouldn't be a good idea to contact the "unknown" people. To quote zoologist Konrad Lorenz: "To kill a culture, it is often sufficient to bring it into contact with another culture, particularly if the latter is higher . . . or at least regarded as higher."

In addition to the killing of cultures, contact can literally kill the people in remote cultures. For example, the Sadlermiut in the Canadian Arctic were a more or less uncontacted group of Inuit who were visited by a British whaling ship in 1902. One of the whalers had a case of influenza or perhaps typhoid fever, and he passed on the disease to the Sadlermiut. Only one woman and four children survived this "contact."

When I told my Danish friend I was backing out of the expedition, he said he was backing out of it, too. His sentiments were exactly the same as mine. "Those people, if they exist, do not deserve to become like us," he said.

So it was that I remained in Angmagssalik, content to document the lore of the locals there. One man I met had a wooden leg that he'd made from the cross-pieces of his dog sled. As a result, he was the most highly regarded craftsperson in the village.

I also met an elderly woman who had fine lines around her eyes from a lifetime of squinting at ice and snow. She informed me that her mother had been a *pujoq* (seal) prior to becoming a human being.

"What kind of seal?" I asked her.

"A Greenland seal [*Pagophilus groenlandicus*], of course," she said with a prideful look on her face.

ᒧᒧᒧᒧ

WHERE THE DEAD MEN REST

With a bonanza of polar bears readily available for touristic photo shoots, Churchill, Manitoba, has been called "The Polar Bear Capital of the World." The Danish explorer Jens Munk once ended up near this present-day tourist mecca not because he wanted to gawk at polar bears, but because he was trying to find the Northwest Passage. His two ships, the frigate *Unicorn* and the sloop *Lamprey*, were forced into an estuary of the Churchill River due to the notoriously unpredictable weather in Hudson Bay.

Just after Munk's arrival in September 1619, the northern winter began its siege. Munk's crew started dying one by one, and by spring of the next year, only Munk himself seemed to be alive. He was expecting his own death when he saw two of his crewmen on the shore. They'd left the boat earlier without his knowing it, and now they helped him off the *Unicorn*, then fed him some of the previous year's berries and plant roots. His health returned, and the three men sailed back to Denmark.

Caused by a Vitamin C deficiency, scurvy was probably the culprit of expedition's poor health. For Munk's men had no access to Vitamin C during their overwintering. In other words, they had no fresh meat (note: raw meat is better than cooked meat as an antiscorbutic), no greens, and no fruit. They might have had medication for their bleeding gums, loose teeth, swollen eyes, and painful joints, but the ship's doctor couldn't read the Latin names in his medical kit.

The sixty-three bodies were either put into unmarked graves near the shore or simply rolled off the ships. A hundred years later, the English explorer James Knight, who was setting up a Hudson Bay Company post at the Munk overwintering site, found numerous "skulls and bones of men." He also noted that "a great many of the graves be under some part of our building."

On a visit to Churchill, I decided to investigate the place where Munk overwintered, so I went across the river with a local guide named Kelsey Eliasson. We put the boat ashore in a small cove, where there was quite a bit of scurvy grass (*Cochlearia offinalis*) near the shore. This is a plant extremely high in Vitamin C that has been eaten or used in a tea to fight off scurvy since Roman times. Apparently, Munk and his men were unaware of this fact.

After tying up the boat, we began searching for rusty pieces of cutlery, the remains of a clay pipe, or perhaps a stray Danish bone. Meanwhile, Kelsey kept his rifle at the ready in case a polar bear showed up and decided that, in the absence of a seal, one of us might make a decent edible.

Soon we found ourselves mired in a dense forest . . . a dense forest of willows two to three feet high. Since we had climbed up a modest slope, we were doubtless above the burial site, so we began climbing down the slope at a different spot than where we'd climbed up.

And then we found . . . berries. Crowberries, bilberries, gooseberries, and salmonberries. Berries galore.

Right away Munk's overwintering became history in our thoughts, and we transformed ourselves into hunter-gatherers. Or I should say hunter-gorgers, since we were now popping huge amounts of berries into our mouths.

I especially looked for cloudberries (*Rubus chamaemorus*), whose name suggests that it possesses a bland, wispy flavor. Quite the contrary. With leaves similar to the leaves of a maple, these bunched amber-colored berries in the Rose family carry a hint of sumptuous decay that suggests a fermented, red-blooded cherry.

Kelsey introduced me to eating the pink flowers of fireweed (*Chamaenerion angustifolium*), the first plant that usually colonizes eroded or waste areas in these parts. Chewing the flowers will ease the discomfort of a sore throat, he told me. Since I didn't have a sore throat, I returned to my cloudberry gorging.

In the end, we didn't find a single Munk artifact or even a sliver of a seventeenth-century Danish bone. I didn't mind, for it's the journey rather than the destination that matters—especially if that journey includes cloudberries.

ᴨᴨᴨ

LEGENDS OF THE LOST

With his two ships the *Albany* and the *Discovery*, Captain James Knight left England in 1719 to search for the Northwest Passage. He decided to overwinter on Marble Island, an uninhabited fastness of white quartzite in western Hudson Bay, because it had the best harbor in those parts. And neither he or his forty crewmen were ever heard from again. Were they killed by Inuit? Assimilated by Inuit? Did they fall through the ice while trying to make it to the mainland?

A while back, I joined Bill Gawor from Rankin Inlet and Fred Ford from Baker Lake on an expedition to Marble Island. We investigated the Knight house site, but found nothing that might have given us a clue about what might have happened to Knight and his men. We searched for but did not find a graveyard, although explorer Samuel Hearne claimed to have found a large one on the island in 1767. At one point Bill found a stanchion of stout English oak that may (or may not) have belonged to one of Knight's ships.

Marble Island's whiteness can easily camouflage a polar bear, with the result that a person might think they're stepping on quartzite, but then that quartzite will rise up and smite them. Thus the three of us carried rifles almost all of the time. At one point I saw a large white form seemingly moving in my direction, and I quickly raised my rifle. The white form turned out to be snow being blown off one of our tents by a typically vigorous Hudson Bay wind.

After a week on the island, we were no closer to solving the Knight mystery than when we arrived, so we decided to call it quits. In the mainland village of Rankin Inlet, I queried Inuit elders about Captain Knight. One of these elders, Ollie Ittinuar, told me a story he'd heard as a young man. Here's an abbreviated version of that story:

In the spring of 1720, a large ship with other *qallunaat* (white men) came to Marble Island just as Knight and his men were getting ready to leave. There was a big battle between the men in the ship and the men on the island. Some of Knight's men were killed during the battle, and the rest were forced aboard the ship, which then sailed away.

Right away this story made me think of the French, who were making sneak attacks on English forts in

Hudson Bay at this time. Let's imagine a French ship, more or less a privateer, arriving on Marble Island . . . and who should the ship's crew encounter but Captain Knight, who'd twice seized forts in Hudson Bay from the French, and George Berley, who'd fought off a French attack on Fort Albany in 1704. The scenario might have been similar to the one Ollie described. Likewise, the remains of the *Discovery* and the *Albany* have been found positioned close together at the bottom of Marble Island's East End Harbor, a fact that might suggest they'd been scuttled by the French.

Ollie said he didn't know where the ship ended up, so I made a few speculations myself. Could it have been wrecked by ice or the notoriously bad weather of Hudson Bay? Could it have transported Knight and his men to North Africa and sold them as slaves to the Berbers, a common practice by French privateers? If this last hypothesis is correct, there might be Algerians or Tunisians today with genes from individuals who overwintered in the Arctic a long time ago.

Questions, questions, questions. As is often the case, the Arctic triumphs over the guesswork of us humans.

ᒧᒪᒧᒪ

ANOTHER MISSING PERSON

Perhaps because he regarded himself as a force of nature, a wealthy, athletic man from upstate New Jersey named Herman Koehler figured he would never have any problem triumphing over the wild Labrador outback. He made two relatively successful trips there, but on his third trip his ego went into overdrive and took its toll.

In the fall of 1931, Koehler was heading north toward the coastal village of Nain with his expedition mate Fred Connell and their guide, a twenty-six-year-old Labrador man named Jim Martin. The local Innu drew a chart for them indicating the proper route via Voisey's Bay on the coast, but Koehler ignored this chart because he had his own not necessarily informed idea about the proper route. Thus the three men set off for the unnavigable Notakwanon River.

Connell's bloated body was found near George River in July of the following year. His face seemed to have been mutilated by foxes. Koehler's own remains weren't discovered until 1938 and consisted of a scattering of bones minus a skull. He'd probably frozen or starved to death and been later eaten by a bear. As for Jim Martin, his body wasn't found, which has led to the following speculations:

- He couldn't tolerate Koehler's dictatorial manner, so he left him and went to live incognito with the Innu.
- A Labrador guide would never leave his client no matter how intolerable that client was, so his bones must still be lying around somewhere.
- He headed for the coast and ended up on Baffin Island, where he became a fur trader under an assumed name.
- He fell through the ice and disappeared forever.
- Being an avid outdoorsman, he lived the remainder of his life in some remote part of the bush.

There has been at least one possible sighting of Jim Martin in relatively recent times. Labrador oral historian Doris Saunders told me that, in 1976, Jim's sister Charlotte was looking out the window of her home on Dumpling Island in Sandwich Bay when she saw a small boat approaching. She got out her spyglass and saw what looked like her brother in the boat. Although he was more than forty years older than when she last saw him, she was certain he was her brother. When he realized that she'd seen him, the man quickly turned the boat around and disappeared around Kettle Cove Head.

In 1991, I heard that Jim Martin had visited a woman who'd been his girlfriend in Cartwright before the Koehler expedition and who now lived just outside the village of Northwest River. This visit had probably taken place some ten years ago, and I heard the former girlfriend was still alive, albeit somewhat ancient.

Being in Northwest River myself, I was eager to talk with this woman, so on a winter day I snowshoed two miles past the leafless skeletons of poplars and birch trees to her home.

Answering my knock, a woman with a supremely weathered face opened the door, then screeched at me, "No tax collectors!"

"I'm not a tax collector," I said. "I just want to know if Jim Martin ever came—"

"Jim Martin? Never heard of 'im!" she screeched again, slamming the door more or less in my face.

Oh well, I thought, it's been nice snowshoeing here, and it'll be nice snowshoeing back to town.

There have been no recent sightings of Jim Martin. Yet such was his delight in being in the Labrador outback that I can almost imagine him still hanging out there, still spry at the age of 115.

ⵎⵎⵎⵎ

A REMARKABLE PIMPLE

A meteorite four hundred feet in diameter whisks through the atmosphere in a fiery flash. Traveling at twenty miles per second, it slams into the earth, sending boulder-sized rocks flying off in all directions as well as excavating a gaping hole in the earth's crust.

Some 1.4 million years later, I was seated in a Twin Otter aircraft flying over northern Quebec's Nunivik region and looking out the window at the seemingly endless tundra. Suddenly I saw a perfectly circular blue eye—the meteorite's crater filled with water. Formerly called Chubb Crater, it now bears the Inuit name Pingualuit, a word that simply means pimple. Being three miles wide, the crater is an unusually large pimple.

Pingualuit is now a national park, and once when I landed on an airstrip near the crater, an Inuk ranger named Yaakaa greeted me and showed me where to pitch my tent.

During my week-long visit, I encountered a totally pristine habitat, with none of the broken-down ATVs, candy bar wrappers, or potato chip bags that litter so many other parts of the Canadian North. Apart from a few old Inuit fox traps, there was no evidence that my litter-minded species had spent any time here.

A few days after my arrival, Yaakaa and I climbed up the slope that led to the crater. This slope was cluttered with the granitic boulders that had been forcibly ejected by the meteorite's original impact. Each of these boulders displayed artwork created by such lichens as the map lichen (*Rhizocarpon geographicum*) and the bright orange sunburst lichen (*Xanthoria elegans*).

After little more than an hour, we were standing at the crater's rim, and I looked down at the huge circular lake that I'd seen from the air. The water was the bluest blue I'd ever seen.

"We call this lake the Crystal Eye of Nunivik," Yaakaa said, "and it may have the purest water of any lake in the world."

We walked around the edge to a spot where the slope down to the lake was the least steep. As we hiked down, the quietude was interrupted by several loud maniacal laughs, followed by a sound similar to an explosion.

I wondered: Was the Crystal Eye laughing at me, an outsider?

Not at all. The inside of the crater was a giant amphitheater, and its walls amplified any sound that occurred inside it. What I heard was a couple of loons chortling at each other and diving for fish. The splashes from their dives were the explosions.

When we reached the bottom, I cupped my hands in the lake, then raised them to my mouth. I tasted a rich, full flavor that made all the other water I'd ever tasted seem tacky as well as downright dull.

As we were hiking back up to the rim, I could still hear the loons screaming *wahoo! quarpp! wahoo wahoo!* Since loons are among the very last birds to migrate south for the winter, they would probably be screaming in this fashion right up until the time the lake froze.

When we reached the top of the crater, I stared one last time at the remarkable blue eye that seemed to be staring directly at me.

ⅎⅎⅎⅎ

AN OUTHOUSE AT THE END OF THE WORLD

Once upon a time I joined a group of Russian scientists on an expedition to Siberia's Wrangel Island. The purpose of our trip was to document the flora, fauna, and fungi on this remote island in the Chukchi Sea. Since Wrangel has the largest density of denning polar bears of anywhere in the world, we were obliged to carry a firearm or a can of Mace with us at all times. Being a lousy shot, I chose the latter.

"You need vodka, too," a Russian botanist informed me, energetically puffing on a Troika cigarette. "Otherwise, you won't be able to identify unusual species." He handed me a 1.75 liter bottle of Hammer & Sickle Vodka.

Here I should mention that Wrangel's landscape was unscathed by Ice Age glaciers, with the result that it looks more or less the same as it looked a million years ago. Endemic species abound. The island boasts twenty-three plant species found nowhere else in the world, and perhaps half as many endemic butterfly species. Small wonder that it's become a UNESCO World Heritage Site.

So there I was, wandering the sedge tundra on the eastern side of the island. In a rocky outcrop, I saw a Muir's fleabane (*Erigerone muirii*), a flowering plant in the aster family first documented by the American naturalist John Muir on an 1881 visit to the island. A short while later, I discovered a small, brownish mushroom, which turned out to be a previously undescribed *Inocybe* species.

Then I saw a heap of polar bear shit festooned with with seal whiskers, berry pits, a delicate maze of birds' bones, and what looked like some kelp. What a splendid work of art! I told myself.

In a short while, a powerful wind called a *yuzhak* began blowing, snarling, and whistling across the tundra. Plants such as cotton grass (*Eriophorum sp.*), bladder campion, and alpine arnica as well as Muir's fleabane sashayed back and forth, repeatedly back and forth, as if they were performing some sort of exotic dance. None of them seemed in danger of being blown down, but I felt I was constantly at risk of being picked up and deposited into the Chukchi Sea.

Suddenly I saw an ATV coming in my direction. An ATV seemingly running on its own, without a driver.

Would Wrangel Island's wonders never cease? Then I saw the botanist who'd given me the vodka hunched low against the vehicle's wheel to escape the blasts of the wind. He saw me and stopped.

"Want to see one of the northernmost outhouses in the world?" he shouted, and then gestured for me to hop into his ATV.

Fifteen minutes later, we reached what turned out to be a lavatorial relic from Soviet times. Its wooden walls had mostly collapsed, its floor was a mass of moss, and its lichen-covered seat was not even a semicircle, much less a circle. What remained was tilted precariously to the starboard. Northernmost outhouse or not, it didn't seem to care about being listed in the Guinness Book of Records. *To hell with celebrity!* its ruinous state seemed to proclaim. *My only wish is to become part of this remote bounteous earth.*

⅃⅂⅃⅂

LIQUID GOLD

I once found myself on northern Vancouver Island's Grease Trail. Contrary to what you might think, this phrase doesn't refer to an itinerary that connects local Burger King, McDonald's, and KFC franchises. Rather, it's the route that 'Namgis First Nation people once used to transport grease across the northern part of the island.

A while back, the grease in question—rendered from a smelt-like fish called the eulachon (*Thaleichthys pacifica*)—was once an extremely valuable trade item. When fresh, it was a highly regarded condiment, and when dried, it would be stuck on a wick and burned like a candle. Those Native people who didn't have access to it eagerly traded items like copper and muskets with those who did, like the 'Namgis. It's possible that the phrase "Oregon Trail" is a corruption of "eulachon trail," for the Oregon Trail was a southerly trade route for the grease.

Eulachon grease is still esteemed by the 'Namgis, who refer to it as "liquid gold." At the instigation of Randy Bell, my 'Namgis host in Alert Bay, I smeared some on smoked salmon and regretted it, for the grease replaced the flavor of the salmon with a flavor not unlike somewhat rancid lard. I continued to eat the smoked salmon, but without the grease.

Undeterred by my negative reaction, Randy offered to show me the highlights of the so-called Grease Trail, including some remarkable petroglyphs carved onto rocks on the opposite side of Woss Lake. So we climbed into his pickup, took the ferry to the town of Port McNeill, and headed into Vancouver Island's northern interior.

Our first stop was another petroglyph site on the shore of the Nimpkish River. Several frowning faces were carved onto a series of boulders, an indication, Randy said, that enemy heads had been severed at this site.

"Did the enemies make disparaging remarks about eulachon grease?" I asked uneasily.

"Not at all." Randy smiled. "The enemies were people from Gilford Island, and we were always fighting with them. We cut off their heads and hung them in that cedar tree above us."

Half expecting to see a collection of weather-worn human heads, I peered up at the tree. There was indeed a head, but it belonged to a bald eagle peering down on me.

"You know why bald eagles' heads are white?" Randy said, then answered the question himself: "Because they're always nesting under ravens." Raven shit is, of course, white—hence this commonly told 'Namgis joke.

A few miles south of Nimpkish Lake, we started hiking along a trail that grease-carrying 'Namgis also would have hiked. Within minutes, the sky opened up, and what cascaded down would have made an Asiatic monsoon seem like a polite drizzle. We hiked on, increasingly waterlogged.

When we returned to the truck, the rain, as if on cue, ceased. We followed a road that meandered along the shore of Woss Lake. A few years ago, Randy said, his truck had broken down not far from here, and he'd had to trek twenty miles in the middle of the night.

At one point he stopped and studied the lake. A strong wind was whipping it in a frenzy. "I'm afraid we can't cross the lake to see the petroglyphs," Randy observed. "It'll just be too dangerous."

"Well, I've already seen some very nice petroglyphs," I said, trying to conceal my disappointment.

As the rain started up again, we continued to drive along the lake. The road grew increasingly muddy. Toward the end of the lake, we came to a halt: a recent avalanche blocked our way. We had no choice but to turn around and, in doing so, miss out exploring the western section of the Grease Trail.

The rain was now coming down even more heavily than before. Suddenly I heard the telltale sound of a flat tire.

Randy now began rummaging under the seat. "Someone seems to have taken my jack," he observed.

Recalling the story of his twenty-mile hike, I had visions of hiking back to Port McNeill while being pummeled to a jellylike consistency by the vehement rain. Randy noticed the troubled look on my face and said, "Trust in serendipity."

"Where are you going?" I shouted. For he'd begun walking briskly away from the truck.

"To get help, Kemosabe," he shouted back, using Tonto's word for the Lone Ranger with a certain jocularity.

Meanwhile the rain was beating a tattoo on the truck, sounding now like buckshot, now like machine-gun fire. I imagined myself being attacked by a hitherto undocumented army of Vancouver Island vigilantes.

Two hours later, another pickup truck splattered up to the one in which I was sitting, and Randy himself climbed out, flashing the victory sign. Another man also climbed out with a jack, so it wasn't long before the stricken tire had been replaced by a new one.

"So how did you know you were going to find help?" I asked Randy.

"I trusted in serendipity," he replied, then pointed to the other man. "Also, my cousin has a cabin down here, and I figured he'd have a jack."

Back in Alert Bay, I smeared eulachon grease on some smoked salmon again. This time the grease had a much better—indeed outdoor—flavor, as if it was permeated with the realm I'd just experienced.

⌐⌐⌐⌐

THE BIGGEST BELLY IN THE WORLD

I was once talking with a Greenlandic schoolteacher as we wandered down the heavily touristed main street of Illulissat, West Greenland. "Because we have so many pretty glaciers, we now have more tourists here than we had *kullut* [lice] in the old days," the man informed me, adding: "But, of course, all our glaciers are melting, so I wonder if the day will soon come when we have no tourists . . ."

I thought I detected a smile on his face when he made this last comment.

We passed slumbering sled dogs being photographed by tourists, who probably didn't realize the dogs had been put there precisely for this purpose. For most Greenlanders now use snow machines, not dog sleds, to get around in the winter.

My companion went on. "The tourists bring us lots of money," he said, "so we don't need to go hunting except in grocery stores, where we hunt for candy bars, hot dogs, soda pop, biscuits, marshmallow cream, and all sorts of processed stuff with carbohydrates and sugars. This sort of hunting makes our people really fat."

"And probably gives a lot of them diabetes, too," I remarked.

"*Aapi.* Especially our *uvikkauniq* [young people]."

"Were there any fat people living here before the tourists came?"

"There was at least one. His name was Atungait, and he was very unusual. I'll tell you about him if you like."

"I'd much rather hear about him than hear about Jens-Erik Kirkegaard, your minister of natural resources. That guy says he likes climate change because it does such a good job of marketing Greenland's natural resources to investors, he doesn't need to do any marketing at all."

"Jens-Erik, he's an *iteq* [asshole]. But Atungait was also an *iteq*. He wouldn't share his food with anyone because he wanted to eat it all himself. And the more he ate, the bigger his belly got, until he needed another place to put his food. What place was big enough? He picked that mountain you see right over there. Now the biggest belly in the whole world was his. He was so proud of this belly that he walked under it all the time.

But a bad thing happened to him one day when he was walking under the mountain—"

All at once he was accosted by an American tourist, who asked him how to get to a particular souvenir shop. The Greenlander gave directions to the tourist, then turned to me and finished his story: "Yes, one day Atunguit was walking under the mountain, and an avalanche came down and killed him . . ."

⎍⎍⎍⎍

REACHING A SUMMIT

Atlin is a former gold-mining town located in the extreme northern part of British Columbia. From the moment I arrived there, I found myself staring at Teresa Island, which, rising 4,567 feet above Atlin Lake, is among the highest inland islands in the world.

The longer I stared at this uninhabited mass of rock and boreal forest, the more I wanted to climb to its summit. After I made a few queries in Atlin, I found just the right person to guide me to the top—an Austrian mountaineer-artist named Gernot Dick.

Gernot agreed to be my guide, and we headed off from the mainland in his motorboat. Once we reached the island, he chose a route that followed a steep avalanche chute on the northwest side. According to Gernot, this route would not only keep us out of the island's virtually impenetrable forests, but it would also give us an opportunity for an advance sighting of any grizzly bear that might be interested in a human meal.

As it happened, our initial ascent took us through what a bear might have regarded as an alfresco restaurant—a dense growth of raspberry bushes. Higher up, we began walking on top of an entire forest of lodgepole pines felled by an avalanche. The footing was precarious. A single false step could mean a sprained ankle or a downward tumble.

Gernot, who was nearly seventy, sprinted over the recumbent trees with the aplomb of a mountain goat. Although much younger, I alternately walked or crawled over those same trees at the speed of a sluggish tortoise.

After we completed our traverse of the fallen forest, we headed up a stream bed created by the summit's melting snow. Occasional patches of ice sent me skidding and sliding in all directions. "Better the sideways path than the straight and narrow one," the mountain seemed to be telling me.

A waterfall now blocked our progress, so we climbed a ridge and scrambled over more fallen trees. Gernot unsheathed his machete and slashed away some of the more recalcitrant branches.

At last we were above tree line and hiking up a slope that stood at an almost vertical tilt with the rest of existence. After an hour or so, we stopped to rest on an incline, and as Gernot played a medley of Tyrolean mountain songs on his harmonica, I gazed out on the world.

Several thousand feet below us, Atlin Lake was an expanse of turquoise that suggested the Mediterranean rather than the Canadian North. Cumulous clouds sailed by overhead like a fleet of luminous cauliflowers. The green of the surrounding forests seemed to surpass any other green I'd ever seen, even in the tropics.

I informed Gernot that I was ready to make the descent.

"You're not interested in reaching the summit?" he said, with a surprised look on his face.

I shook my head. For I couldn't imagine the summit offering me as wondrous a view as the place where I was now seated. Also, I had the distinct impression that Teresa Island wanted to be alone now—alone with its waterfalls, its fallen trees, its raspberry bushes, and perhaps even a few bears, but without a pair of human invaders.

And so, we started down.

⌐_⌐_

FARTHEST NORTH

As the northernmost town in the world, Longyearbyen (pop. 1,500) in Norway's Svalbard archipelago boasts the world's northernmost Thai massage parlor, the world's northernmost kabob wagon, and the world's northernmost pizza parlor. Rather than sample these attractions, I decided to investigate the realm beyond the scree slopes that surrounded the town.

So it was that my Norwegian friend Sven-Erik and I began climbing a nearby mountain called Platåberget. Sven-Erik had a 30.06 rifle slung over his shoulder. For Svalbard's polar bears sometimes seek out members of our species as a dietary supplement to seal meat, and if a person is carrying a heavy gauge rifle, he or she can usually keep these white-clad diners at a distance.

We climbed the mountain, and when we reached its flat summit, we saw pools of meltwater, stunted plants, and an abundance of lichen-decorated rocks. Certainly, there wasn't enough snow for a snowmobile—an extremely popular item in Svalbard. So why did I seem to be hearing one?

As it happened, I was hearing the ringtone of Sven-Erik's cellphone. He'd programmed it to sound like the exhaust sound of a snowmobile. "*Ja*," he told his wife. "Of course, I have my rifle with me."

Up and down various rocky slopes we hiked. At one point we came to a stone cairn, the so called Ninavarden (Nina Memorial). It was here in 1995 that a young Norwegian woman named Nina Olaussen was killed and eaten by a mountain-climbing polar bear. She loved all wild creatures and assumed all wild creatures would love her. One such creature did in fact love her . . . to death.

"Was Nina carrying a firearm?" I asked Sven-Erik.

"*Nei*," he replied.

Our own trip included no wild creatures, either in attack mode or otherwise, except a few ravens, a few fluttering snow buntings, and a vole. Nor were there any fear-invoking moments, though we did have a pissed off moment when we saw a batch of Carlsberg lager cans wedged between some boulders.

We continued climbing, then glissaded down a crevasse, hiked along a valley, and then wandered into Huset, doubtless the northernmost bar-restaurant in the world. It looked no different from any other establishment of its kind except for the gun rack in its vestibule.

Sven-Erik and I toasted each other with glasses of Gilde, a sweet-tasting Norwegian aquavit. Then he went home, and I decided to do a bit more exploring. I was walking toward the burial ground for the northernmost victims of the 1918 Spanish flu epidemic when a large white form emerged from a culvert.

My heart skipped a beat, then skipped a second beat because I wasn't carrying a rifle. But the white form turned out not to be a polar bear, but one of Svalbard's reindeer still wearing its winter coat. Soon the animal was grazing on clumps of *Cladonia* lichen growing next to the cross of one of the flu victims.

I assuaged my skipped heartbeats by heading back to Huset and drinking another, no, two more glasses of aquavit. Seated next to me at the bar was a Norwegian lady who periodically bent over and offered tidbits of food to a small mass of white. She wasn't feeding a baby polar bear or an infant reindeer, but doubtless the northernmost toy poodle in the world.

ICELANDIC NOTES

As a vehement wind constructs hock and tongue on the snowed-up ground, two farm-bodied girls hold hands and happily dance with the already dancing snowflakes.

A farmer named Sigurdur told me he was looking for lost sheep when he met a tall, gray-faced man who looked hungry. He offered this fellow some *hangkjot* (smoked lamb) and a knife to cut it with. "*Nej, thokk fyrir*," said the man, taking off his head and tilting it politely, "We *draugur* [ghosts] don't need knives."

In the Reykjavík phone directory, there are numerous individuals named Raven (Hrafn), Eagle (Orn), Swallow (Thröstur), Bear (Bjorn), and Lonesome Rider (Indridi), but there are only two Cuckoos (Gaukur).

Remarked the fisherman: "You know where halibut come from? Years ago Jesus Christ spat, and from his spittle came that fish. Nothing else Jesus ever did was nearly so useful."

In a scraggly field of lava near Mount Herðubreið squats an Isuzu Trooper splattered with raven shit, each gob of which proclaims, "Take that, you damn intruder!"

I was walking along a road in the Westfjords when a car stopped, and the driver, an Englishman, asked me if I wanted a lift. Then he sniffed the not necessarily pleasant odor of the *hákarl* (fermented shark's meat) I had in my rucksack and said, "Good God, man, have you robbed a graveyard?" And quickly drove off.

Weird gleams just before midnight in Hjalteyri—the moon reflecting off the dead eyes of cod hung up to dry.

ᴍᴍᴍ

EAST GREENLAND NOTES

Every once in a while, a vehement *piteraq* wind will blow out half the windows in the village of Tasiilaq. I find it difficult not to admire something so completely indifferent to human endeavor.

In Sermiligaaq, an elder flushed a toilet, then flushed it again. "White man's toy," he declared, then happily squatted on his chamber pot.

Grains of snow hard enough to draw blood—the fluffy stuff from down south, by comparison, is wimpish.

The slime from a walrus hide garnished with human urine was once thought to be a delicacy, an old East Greenlandic woman informed me, adding that, like most fine food, you can't find it in the local markets.

Lengthy floating cirrus clouds are the skeleton of a whale transported to the sky but still swimming, say East Greenlanders, adding that whales are such hardy animals, they never completely disappear.

According to the elder in Sermiligaaq, *angakut* (shamans) were once able to yank off a person's genitals, toss them high in the air, catch them, and stick them back on the person, no problem. No modern doctor can do this, the man observed.

Such was the elegance of the serried ridges directly in front of me that I imagined they had been squeezed from putty by an artistically inclined sky god and flung down to the earth, where they hardened.

ᴖᴖᴖᴖ

THE BOYS OF WINTER

On the Yukon's Herschel Island, I once found the badly weathered handle of a baseball bat lying on the island's southern shore. A hundred feet away, I found the business end either of that same bat or another one.

Lying two hundred miles north of the Arctic Circle in the Yukon, Herschel Island would seem to be an unlikely setting for the great American pastime. For one thing, it snows there every month of the year. For another, there's hardly anywhere on the island flat enough for a ball field. Even so, this chunk of tundra once had its own highly competitive baseball league— the most wintry of all winter leagues.

During the 1890s, Arctic whaling ships spent their winter frozen in at Herschel's Pauline Cove instead of steaming back to San Francisco or New England. By doing this, a captain could lengthen his harvest of bowhead and other types of baleen whales by at least a month and also get a jump on the ships coming up from the south the next spring.

But staying the winter on Herschel meant killing time for seven or so solid months. The whalers needed some sort of diversion so they wouldn't drink themselves into a prolonged stupor, desert their ships, or spend their time compromising the virtues of not necessarily virtuous Inuvialuit women on Qiqiqtaruk (the Inuvialuit name for Herschel). This last activity earned Herschel the nickname "Sodom and Gomorrah of the Ice-Fields."

When in early 1894 a few bats and balls were discovered in the hold of the barkentine named the *Newport*, the first mate of that ship, Hartson Bodfish, decided to turn Pauline Cove's frozen surface into a ball field. Ash from the ship's furnace marked the baselines. An old sail became the backstop. And on February 19, 1894, probably the first baseball game in the Arctic was played—officers versus crew. The temperature at game time stood at −20°F.

There was such enthusiasm among the whalers after this first chilly contest that a four-team league was immediately formed. The teams were named the Arctics, the Northern Lights, the Herschels, and the Pickups. Rules decreed that each game be played "regardless of weather."

Because of irregularities in the field such as ice hummocks and frost heaves, the games were unusually high scoring, with balls ricocheting off in all directions.

On March 13, 1894, the newly formed Nonpareils (who replaced the Pick-ups) beat the Herschels 81–12. They beat the Herschels again on April 20, though the score was much closer, 38–31. Then on May 4 the Herschels walloped the Arctics 85–10. They also bashed the Northern Lights 37–6 and 25–3. ("The Northern Lights," Captain George Leavitt wrote in his log, "are a darn poor club.") The Nonpareils were the winners of the first annual Arctic Whalemen's Pennant, a piece of canvas nailed to a broomstick.

The whalers took their baseball seriously. On April 11, 1895, a disagreement over where to lay out the diamond on Pauline Cove resulted in the fatal stabbing of one whaler by another. And on March 1, 1896, a Sunday, Captain Albert C. Sherman of the *Beluga* reported in his log: "Four degrees above zero. A large crowd on the baseball field, but as usual a small one in the church." Games were interrupted only when someone yelled, "Polar bear in the outfield!"

The following year the Arctic took its revenge on those who presumed to sport in its territory. March 7 started out unseasonably mild, only a degree or two below freezing. A game had progressed to the bottom of the second inning when a blizzard struck. Visibility was nonexistent. By the time the storm passed, three of the players had frozen to death. Imagine a captain saying to a widow, "I'm sorry, my dear, but your husband froze to death in the bottom of the second inning."

Another man, a Norwegian crewman playing in the outfield, was able to crawl back to the *Wanderer*, where the ship's crew chipped fifteen pounds of ice from the hood of his parka. This act had to be done very carefully, lest not only the ice but also pieces of the crewman's head be chipped away.

It wasn't long before both whaling and Herschel Island baseball gave up the ghost, for women had lost interest in having an eighteen-inch waist. To achieve that measurement, the whalebone corset had been the garment of choice. But by the early twentieth century, stiff corsets were a thing of the past. Bowheads and other types of whales had almost become things of the past themselves, since they'd been hunted nearly to extinction. Fur trading replaced whaling as an economic activity, but in the 1930s the fur trade collapsed, and Herschel reverted to its former status as an Arctic backwater.

Today Herschel is not even a backwater. Nobody lives year-round on the island, which is now a Yukon Territorial Park. Those few visitors who find their way to Herschel each year see the ghosts of time: rusting metal, boats left high and dry, abandoned buildings, and pushed-up coffins. A colony of black guillemots often nests among the rafters of the old Anglican church. Rising sea levels, which have caused considerable shoreline erosion, might sweep this church into the Beaufort Sea in the not too distant future.

During my visit to Herschel, I occasionally would hear the crack of a calving iceberg. This crack would be not unlike the reverberation of a bat hitting a baseball—a sound that would have split the local air over a century earlier. With the warming of the Arctic, these cracks are occurring less and less frequently. I suspect it won't be long before they become like baseball on Herschel Island, a thing of the past.

⅃⌐⌐⌐⌐

HELL ANIMAL

Some years ago, I was getting into a kayak in Tasiilaq, East Greenland, when a local man walked over to me. "You mustn't let a *tupilak* tip over your kayak!" he said. He laughed, then opened his mouth wide and closed it quickly to indicate what would happen to me if I ran afoul of a *tupilak*.

I'd already seen a *tupilak* in Tasiilaq. Dozens of *tupilaks*, in fact. While none of them made an effort to dine on me, their eagerly dangling tongues suggested they would have been happy to do so.

The first outsider to document *tupilaks* in East Greenland was Captain Gustav Holm of the Royal Danish Navy, who visited the area around Tasiilaq in 1884. Holm described an *angakok* (shaman) who attached the jawbone of a fox and a ptarmigan's feathers to a dead child's body, then brought this creation alive by simultaneously chanting and having it suckle his genitals. Once alive, it became a *tupilak*, whereupon its creator would send it off to dispose of an enemy, often by yanking out that enemy's entrails and eating them.

A *tupilak* couldn't locate its target unless something belonging to that target was included among its ingredients—a kayak sleeve, some hairs, a fingernail, or perhaps a piece of clothing. If the bones of a seal were also included, the *tupilak* would swim toward its victim; if bird bones were used, it would fly after its victim. One particular *tupilak* had an infant's skull affixed to a sandpiper's skeleton, and it flew down to the woman who was the *angakok*'s intended victim and literally fed on her breast, yanking it off and eating it.

What I've just described may seem like the stuff of horror movies, but it's also the stuff of anthropological inquiry. In 1905, the Danish ethnographer William Thalbitzer visited East Greenland and met the celebrated *angakok* Missuarniannga, whose name means "Suck Me." In response to Thalbitzer's question about the morphology of *tupilaks*, Missuarniannga carved a nasty-looking figure out of driftwood and stuck several human bones onto it.

After Thalbitzer's visit, other ethnographers came to East Greenland and wanted to see *tupilaks*, too. Soon the demand exceeded the supply of ingredients, so *angakoks* began creating carvings out of sperm whale and walrus teeth as well as the bones of animals. Thus a new version of what explorer-raconteur Peter Freuchen called "the hell animal of East Greenland" was born. This version still came alive by sucking its carver's genitals. It was just as grotesque, too. An example: a female *tupilak* with a bird's beak instead of a topknot, ankle-dragging breasts with fangs, and giant claws in lieu of legs.

Forward to the 1960s. As Christianity's foothold in East Greenland became increasingly secure, and Protestant ministers replaced *angakoks*, *tupilaks* ended up killing fewer and fewer individuals. Even so, they were still being carved, since Denmark, which owned Greenland, had decided to make that capacious island pay for all the kroner being poured into it. One way to do this was to sell Greenlandic handicrafts abroad. Carve *tupilaks*! Danes instructed East Greenlanders.

Nowadays Tasiilaq has a sizable workshop called Stunk where *tupilaks* are produced with electric machinery. Most of the ones I saw in the workshop were remarkably similar in their grotesquerie—they had fat dangling tongues, protruding fangs, and elongated heads that suggested Marfan syndrome in extremis. I dare say not a single one of them would have been capable of yanking out an entrail, but they were extremely proficient at yanking money from a tourist's wallet.

Upon seeing these mass-produced artifacts, I couldn't help but think they were the consequence of Missuarni-annga's having violated a time-honored East Greenland taboo: you mustn't show a magical object to an outsider, or that object will lose all its magic.

Let me conclude by saying that, for better or perhaps for worse, no *tupilak* tipped over my kayak and then tried to yank out my entrails during my visit to Tasiilaq.

ⅎⅎⅎ

VIKING INVADERS

Until the early years of the twentieth century, the only way to reach the island of Grimsey, Iceland's northernmost inhabited place, was by a mail boat that sailed twice a year from the mainland. At most twice a year. There's a story about a Danish visitor who couldn't leave Grimsey, for one storm after another roared down from the Arctic and kept him stuck on the island. At last he gave up and married a local woman. It's said that they lived happily ever after.

I first traveled to Grimsey myself in 1985 when it was still more or less unvisited by tourists. Thirty years later, I traveled again to the island and had the following not necessarily happy experience:

One summer evening I was seated by one of the island's brackish ponds and watching a red-necked phalarope (*Phalaropsis lobatus*) stir up plankton for its supper with its needlelike bill. All of a sudden I heard a barrage of voices. I looked up and saw a crowd of Vikings noisily ambling along a nearby road. Some of the men were wearing horned helmets, some had long gray beards glued to their chins, and some seemed to be dressed in armor. A few of the women were wearing long cloaks with brooches. A Viking in a wheelchair was waving a large sword.

As it happened, these individuals were passengers on a National Geographic cruise ship. They were dressed as Vikings even though Vikings never visited Iceland. The island's early settlers were Norse, not those swash-bucklers who liked nothing better than to reduce a European city to rubble. Although they didn't seem inclined to reduce Grimsey to rubble, these cruise ship Vikings' shouts and guffaws did violate the evening's quietude. Meadow pipits, snow buntings, and northern wheatears flew away. The phalarope quickly stopped churning up plankton, and it flew away, too.

I decided to follow the group even though I wasn't dressed as a marauding Viking. After fifteen minutes, we arrived at our destination—a sign that indicated the Arctic Circle. The sign had arrows pointing in the direction of various cities (London, 1,972 km; Paris, 2,335 km; Rome, 3,436 km; New York, 4,448 km; Sydney, 16,137 km). Out came the Vikings' cameras, as well as their cellphones with selfie attachments.

There was a three-hole basaltic golf course next to the sign. Clubs and golf balls were rented from a nearby guesthouse so that a visitor could tell his or her friends, "Hey, I hit a golf ball across the Arctic Circle!" At least half of the would-be Vikings now started playing this somewhat reduced form of golf. One man swung his club so hard that his helmet went flying through the air and landed in the lap of the Viking in the wheelchair.

Then came the retreat to the cruise ship. Some of the passengers were now holding their helmets in their hands, others were ripping off their fake beards, and still others had taken off their plastic armor. A woman collapsed her foldable sword and put it in her purse. A man replaced his horned helmet with a New York Yankees baseball cap.

This raid wasn't really serious, I told myself. After all, none of the houses on the island were burned down, nor did the invaders injure, much less slaughter a single local inhabitant of Grimsey. Even so, I wondered whether the red-necked phalarope I saw would ever return to the island.

ᴙᴑᴚᴑᴚ

A NORTHERN HOLOCAUST

The Alutiiq village of Old Harbor lies in the southwestern part of Alaska's Kodiak Island. I found the Alutiiq (sometimes called "Pacific Eskimos") to be a cheerful people except when I mentioned Refuge Rock, which they call *Awa'aq*—"the place not to speak of." For on August 14, 1784, a boat carrying a Russian merchant-adventurer named Grigory Shelikhov and his cannoneers killed perhaps a thousand Alutiiq who had sought refuge on this rocky island. The survivors were forced to become slaves of the Russian *promyshlenniks* (fur hunters).

The overwhelming stench of corpses immediately made Refuge Rock uninhabitable. It has remained uninhabited to this very day.

I tried to find someone who would take me to the site of where this northern holocaust occurred. No one seemed willing.

"Too many ghosts," one Alutiiq man said, adding, "I think of it as our Wounded Knee."

"The last time I went there, I heard the weeping of my ancestors," another told me. "I don't want to hear them weeping again."

At last an Alutiiq man named Jeff Peterson offered me the services of his stepson Nolan as my guide. In his boat, Jeff dropped us off at Fox Lagoon on nearby Sitkalidak Island, and Nolan and I began walking along the shore. It was a dismal, intermittently rainy day, which seemed appropriate. For there are certain places where the weather ought to be gloomy, like the place where we were headed.

At last we reached Refuge Rock. Shaped like a recumbent whale and rising a hundred or so feet out of the water, it was joined to Sitkalidak Island by a narrow spit of land buried at high tide. The tide was now low, so we had no trouble walking to our destination.

For an hour, we explored this historic chunk of geology, walking around the base and then clambering up one of its cliffs until we reached its sedge-tousled crown. All around me was a veritable bounty of seabirds—gulls, horned puffins, rhinoceros auklets, goldeneyes, eiders, and fork-tailed storm petrels.

Archaeologists have found numerous artifacts here—spears, charms, slate end blades, ulu blades, and—not surprisingly—human remains. Nolan said this place "freaked" him out.

Let me confess that Refuge Rock didn't freak me out, though the light mist rising from the water in diaphanous wreaths struck me as being a bit ghostly. I didn't hear any ancestral weeping, only the occasional caterwauling of the gulls and squabbling of the eider ducks. But there was no reason why the departed spirits of the Alutiiq should reveal themselves to me, a White Person. For I was, after a fashion, the bringer of their tears.

ᒥᒧᒥᒧ

Miscellaneous
Encounters

AN EXPEDITION CRUISE

The loss of sea ice has been a veritable boon to Arctic cruise companies. In 2015, a thirteen-deck cruise ship named the *Crystal Serenity* journeyed from Vancouver, British Columbia, to New York City and en route traversed the Northwest Passage without a single travail. Too bad, I thought. For travails indicate the triumph of nature over human maneuvers.

Eight years before the *Crystal Serenity*'s voyage, I was a lecturer on a much smaller ship, a Russian vessel named the *Lyubov Orlova* chartered by the now defunct Canadian company Cruise North. I'm happy to report that our trip up the coast of Labrador and beyond consisted primarily of travails.

Toward the beginning of the journey, we began seeing increasingly large ice floes due to the fact of a strong easterly wind pushing all the ice westward. At the sight of a large ice floe or an iceberg, one of the Russian crew members would shout "*Titanic!*"

Given that ice was hugging the coast, the *Orlova* couldn't land at its first two destinations, the Labrador villages of Makkovik and Hopedale. The next day we learned that we wouldn't be landing in Nain, an Inuit community that had prepared a feast of traditional food for us.

I expected to hear lots of grumbling from the passengers, but there was hardly any. "This is the Arctic," observed one of the passengers, "so we've got to the roll with the punches. And this might be our last chance to experience sea ice."

Our next destination was the abandoned Moravian village of Hebron. We went to bed two miles from Hebron and woke up the following morning more than five miles from it because of the ice's capricious movements. In fact, some of us didn't need to wake up, since the constant crunching and grinding of the ice against the ship's hull made sleep virtually impossible.

The *Orlova*'s captain, Andrey Rudenko, gave up on Hebron and decided to head toward the Torngat Mountains National Park some forty miles north of where we were situated. The report from the Canadian Ice Service turned out not to be good, and Captain Rudenko decided it would be best to give a pass to this destination, too.

To my surprise, most of the passengers were also philosophical about not visiting the Torngat Mountains

National Park, which had been advertised as the highlight of the trip. "After all, this trip was billed as an *expedition* cruise," remarked one of the passengers, "and it has really become one."

Next came another travail. At the northern tip of Labrador, we were supposed to visit Killiniq, a village abandoned by its Inuit inhabitants in 1978. Satellite images showed a forty-five-mile-wide band of ice hugging our destination, so Captain Rudenko had no choice but to turn the *Orlova*'s bluff bow east in an effort to reach open water.

For the passengers, the focus of the trip had shifted to the ice itself—its various shapes and forms as well as its beauty. This beauty could be breathtaking, as when the sunset would turn the ice into a shimmering kaleidoscope of orange and red.

One day passed, then another, during which we lecturers regaled the passengers with presentations. One of my lectures was about how Arctic ice acts as the earth's air conditioner, and how its disappearance is turning the planet into a veritable sauna. None of the passengers said, "Hey, look outside, and tell me the ice is disappearing," although one of them did say she thought the ice was attacking our cruise because of what we humans were doing to it.

At last, seemingly free of ice, the ship began moving west toward Ungava Bay. We were now in the apparent home stretch of our journey, but our difficulties weren't over. Captain Rudenko had received a report that there was a barrier of ice in the vicinity of Kuujjuaq, our port of disembarkation in Ungava Bay. He decided to head north to Baffin Island's Frobisher Bay, where there seemed to be less ice.

After a day at sea, we saw the mountains of Baffin Island, and then we were steaming into Frobisher Bay— actually, not steaming into it. Ice conditions had changed dramatically since Captain Rudenko had received the report, and there now seemed to be as much ice there as on the Labrador coast. The captain radioed a Canadian government icebreaker and asked for help. When the icebreaker showed up well after midnight, everyone gathered on the deck and cheered its arrival.

Even while we were still at sea, the passengers were working on stories they would tell their friends back home. Stories that included statements like "I felt like we were seeing an endangered species . . . and sometimes getting stuck in it."

When the *Orlova* came within a few miles of its new port of disembarkation, Nunavut's capital Iqaluit, our adversary decided to give us a goodbye gift. Our zodiacs couldn't find a passage through the ice that was hugging the shore, so we ended up landing several miles from Iqaluit and going there—actually, bouncing there—over the roadless tundra in buses.

In Iqaluit, I found myself talking with an old friend. "So, the trip didn't go according to plan?" he asked.

"Not at all!" I replied enthusiastically.

ᴖᴖᴖᴖ

A VINTAGE ENCOUNTER

On a small island in the southwestern corner of Hudson Bay, my Cree guide Jack and I were cooking a moose stew when I heard the telltale sound of a plane overhead.

Soon the plane, a twin-engine Cessna, was circling our camp. Uh-oh, I thought, here comes trouble. This was a guilt reflex, of course. The same guilt reflexes a person might have at the unexpected appearance of a policeman.

All at once the plane banked. The next thing I knew, its pontoons were plowing through the water a hundred or so feet from our island. Then three men dressed to the teeth and wearing hip waders jumped out and splashed toward the shore. One of them walked up to us and bowed slightly. "May we join you?" he inquired.

Travel is a realm of improbable encounters. The more remote the setting, the more improbable those encounters seem to be. Our visitors turned out to be a group of Italian aristocrats. One was a count, another a duke with an estate outside Verona, and the one who'd just spoken to us introduced himself as a king.

"Are you *really* a king?" I asked doubtfully.

"Yes," the fellow replied. "I'm the elevator king of northern Italy. I make elevators for all the large office buildings there."

Each year, the elevator king told us, the three of them chartered a plane and visited a different remote part of the world. The previous year, they'd hopped around the Brazilian Amazon. The year before, Madagascar. And this year it happened to be the Canadian North. Whenever they saw a camp like ours, they would drop down from the sky and investigate it.

I felt like I was meeting the cast of a Fellini movie.

The elevator king pointed to our stewpot and asked what kind of meat we were cooking.

"Moose," I told him.

"*Alce americano*," he told the others, who apparently didn't speak English. Then he asked me what kind of wine we were drinking with the moose.

He looked stunned when I said we had no wine in our camp. When he translated this for the others, they looked stunned, too.

Even as we spoke, their Canadian pilot was bringing ashore several bottles of wine, along with a pot, a cookstove, and a checkered tablecloth. Then the duke and the count began cooking up some pasta.

While we were eating our respective meals, the elevator king asked Jack if he lived in a tent or a teepee. After all, Native people invariably lived in such traditional structures. Jack shook his head. "I have a house in Peawanuck on the mainland, maybe forty clicks east from here," he said.

"Does your house have running water and electricity?" the elevator king asked.

"Of course," Jack observed, with a grin. "My house also has a TV and a computer. Actually, two computers, since my wife and I each have one."

The elevator king translated this for the others. They seemed a bit surprised by the TV and the computers, but not nearly as surprised as they were by the absence of wine in our camp. They even gave us several bottles of wine, both red and white, to remedy our bereft state.

After they finished their dinner, our visitors shook hands with us, donned their waders, and splashed back to the plane. With props whirling in a haze of oily fumes, the twin-engine Cessna roared across the water, then lifted off into the slate-gray sky, going higher and higher, until it disappeared.

If travel is a realm of improbable encounters, this one seemed more improbable than most. Later, in fact, I found myself wondering whether I'd imagined the whole thing. Then I noticed a few strands of pasta lying on the island's glacial till. In this boreal setting, they seemed like artifacts as extraordinary as any an archaeologist ever dreamed of.

ᴨᴨᴨᴨ

COLD COMFORT

The Norwegian Paul Bjorvig (1857–1935) usually isn't considered an explorer, yet compared with some of the individuals on whose expeditions he took part, he was very much an explorer. An explorer who accepted his trials and tribulations naturally, as if they were an intrinsic part of the Arctic. What follows is the best known of those tribulations.

In 1898, Bjorvig signed on as an ice pilot for a North Pole expedition led by two unlikely Americans, a Chicago journalist named William Wellman and a Missouri alcoholic named Evelyn Baldwin. The expedition used Russia's remote Franz Josef Land as a base camp to reach the Pole, but the leaders spent most of their time roaming the archipelago and giving (in the words of Wellman) "islands, straights, and points good American names." For some reason, they thought Russian names were inappropriate for a Russian locale.

While the two leaders were engaged in their roaming, Bjorvig and another Norwegian, Bernt Bentsen, remained in an ice cave in a place named Fort McKinley (the US president was then William McKinley) and looked after the expedition's supplies. A team of sled dogs shared the cave and sometimes used it, not to mention the two men's sleeping bags, for their lavatorial needs.

This habitation was only forty miles southeast from one of the ice caves explorer Fridtjof Nansen had shared with his expedition mate Hjalmar Johansen a few years earlier. In fact, Bentsen had spent three previous years in the Siberian Arctic on Nansen's ship the *Fram*, but his quarters on that well-known polar vessel were luxurious compared to the ice cave he shared with Bjorvig.

Having become increasingly ill, probably from scurvy, Bentsen died in January 1899. His last request to Bjorvig was to keep a polar bear from eating his remains. Bjorvig promised he would honor this request.

As it happened, the only way to keep a polar bear from eating Bentsen was to keep his body in the ice cave. So Bjorvig wrapped the body in Bentsen's sleeping bag and, because the cave was so small, he was obliged to keep the sleeping bag next to his own. He also felt obliged to keep the sled dogs from regarding Bentsen's body as cuisine.

Meanwhile, Baldwin was drinking himself into a state of stupefaction in the crude Masonic lodge he'd recently constructed. Why construct a Masonic Lodge in Franz Josef Land? Because Baldwin thought it would be popular with his Masonic brothers who might visit these parts.

As for Wellman, he returned to Fort McKinley in the spring. Upon entering the ice cave, he asked: "Where's Bentsen?"

"Dead," Bjorvig replied, pointing to the sleeping bag. Then he offered Wellman a cup of coffee. Later he buried Bentsen's body under a nearby pile of rocks.

When Bjorvig returned to Norway, the media paid almost no attention to the fact that he'd overwintered with a corpse. Nowadays, of course, reporters would be stabbing microphones in his face, asking him questions like "Did your dead bedfellow's smell interfere with your appetite?"

If he'd been asked that sort of question, Bjorvig might have replied: "The important thing was honoring my friend's last request." Then he might have uttered these words, which he subsequently wrote in his journal after describing several more of the tribulations bequeathed to him by cold places: "If a man has no sorrows, he has no joys."

ⁿⁿⁿⁿ

REMEMBERING ELLIOTT MERRICK

My friend Elliott Merrick died on April 22, 1997, less than three weeks before his ninety-second birthday. Toward the end of his life, he remarked that he'd grown so old that he was now "historical."

Bud, as he was known to his friends, turned his back on his upper middle-class background in Montclair, New Jersey, by signing on as a summer Worker Without Pay with Labrador's Grenfell Mission. He soon fell in love with Labrador ("that pristine, beautiful land," he called it) and stayed on as a schoolteacher in North West River. He also fell in love with and married the mission's resident nurse, the tough-minded Kate Austen, whom he sometimes referred to as "Cast-Iron Kate, the Boiler-Maker's Mate."

Perhaps the highlight of Bud's Labrador years was a winter trip he and Kate took with trapper John Michelin. From North West River, the threesome journeyed by canoe and portage up the Grand (now the Churchill) River, then continued by snowshoe and toboggan deep into the bush. Altogether, they covered more than three hundred miles in a mostly unexplored wilderness. In his journal, Bud wrote, "We have traveled to the earth's core and found meaning."

The Merricks returned to the United States in the early 1930s. "The day I left Labrador was the saddest of my life," Bud told me, adding, "A major in English from Yale hardly prepared me for a trapper's life." Eventually, they bought an old farm in Vermont's Northeast Kingdom, one of the few parts of the country that could ever be mistaken for boreal Labrador.

His first book, *True North*, was published in 1933. This account of his trip with John Michelin so enthralled the Scribner's editor, the legendary Maxwell Perkins, that he reputedly asked Bud if there was anything *he* could do in Labrador. The book is a *Walden* of the North, its lyrical, curmudgeonly voice now celebrating Labrador's boreal wilderness, now inveighing against the urban absence of wilderness.

Drawing on Kate's experiences as a Labrador nurse, Bud subsequently wrote *Northern Nurse* (1942), which is among the best books about a woman living in the North—or at least one of the best books about a woman's life in the North written by a man. For this book, he spent so many hours writing notes at Kate's dictation until, he told me, "she wanted to kill me."

Bud was not only a staunch, but also a quite witty traditionalist. For example, I once wrote him about a pair of neoprene-and-aluminum snowshoes I'd worn on a winter trip to Labrador. He wrote back: "I have invented a snowshoe far superior to your aluminum ones. Its frames are composed of an old garden hose, which bends readily, taking either the bear paw shape or that of the Alaska tundra runner. Crossbars are of Victorian corset stays bound together with baling wire, and the mesh is of state-of-the-art chicken wire layered in an intricate pattern. I am depending on you as a qualified expert to see that my creation is installed in the Smithsonian's Hall of Artifacts."

I consider myself fortunate to have been among the handful of people who were Bud's wandering eyes and ears in his last years. If I encountered something unusual on a trip to Labrador, I'd tell myself, wait until Bud hears about *this*! And when I got home, I'd ring him up. He would query me closely about my experiences, and maybe tell me that he knew the deserted

Native camp I'd visited when it was still inhabited some sixty years earlier. Sometimes I'd even hear the rustling of a map in the background.

Bud may or may not have been living vicariously through these conversations with me. One thing I do know: without him as an invisible sidekick, my own journeys in the North have become lonelier.

⌐┌┐┐

AT THE GRAVE OF A MORAVIAN ESKIMO CHIEFTAIN

Born in the Czech region of Moravia in 1868, Jan Welzl was a master fabricator in his books about the Arctic. In the most popular of those books, *Thirty Years in the Golden North*, he claims that Eskimos in the New Siberian Islands had elected him their chieftain—though the New Siberian Islands never had any Eskimo inhabitants. Never any year-round inhabitants, in fact. In another work, *The Quest for Polar Treasure*, he describes thirty-six-foot-tall freshwater octopi whose favorite occupation is killing unwary members of our own species.

Whether Welzl actually visited the places he described in his books is hard to say. But there was one northern place he did visit: the town of Dawson in Canada's Yukon Territory. Not only did he visit it, but he spent the last sixteen years of his life there. While other Dawsonites were searching for gold, Welzl occupied himself in the creation of a perpetual motion machine from old beer cans and bicycle parts. To individuals who visited his cabin, he would point to the machine and, in broken English, say, "She go up, she go down, she go 'yah, yah, yah!'"

Welzl also regaled Dawsonites who visited his cabin with stories about his experiences in the North. For instance, he would allude to his discovery of a race of pygmy Eskimos who'd arrived in Siberia on a meteor from Mars. Or he'd say that kangaroos would make better sled animals than dogs—a pity there were so few of them in the Arctic. He died in 1948, not as a result of an attack by a giant octopus but from a heart attack.

Welzl is the reason so many Czechs visit Dawson as tourists and often end up living there. For he became an iconic figure in their Soviet-run, perhaps Soviet-ruined, country in the 1950s. In their minds, he pursued the life of his choice, without any rules imposed on him by officialdom. And in passages like the following one, from *Thirty Years in the Golden North*, he seems to be criticizing Soviet rule of Czechoslovakia well before that rule existed: "There is true liberty up North. Nobody is limited in his freedom. . . . Whatever you see, you can go after. . . . There is nothing to stop you."

The so called Velvet Revolution put an end to Soviet rule in the Czech Republic, but not an end to the Czech enthusiasm for Jan Welzl. In his home town of Zábřeh, the statue of Stalin was torn down, and a statue of Welzl was placed on the same pedestal Uncle Joe had previously occupied. Likewise, a Prague astronomer named an asteroid (no. 15425) after this eccentric fellow.

Whether locals or tourists, Czechs have long been making pilgrimages to Welzl's grave in Dawson's Catholic cemetery. When I visited the grave myself in 1992, a boot had been placed on it, doubtless a tribute to Welzl's wandering habit. But the cross I saw turned out not to mark Welzl's grave. Apparently, an early Czech visitor had looked for Welzl's grave and, unable to find it, wrote "Jan Welzl" on an unmarked cross. Welzl's admirers were probably laying their wreaths on the grave of an itinerant Italian laborer named Peter Fagetti.

Shortly after my initial visit, Welzl's actual burial place was discovered and duly consecrated on July 24, 1994. A few years ago, I visited this new grave with one of the Czech Dawsonites who helped construct it.

"We created the grave out of a combination of cement and Czech beer," he informed me, adding, with a touch of Welzlian wit, "We considered sticking a radio tube into the grave because this would make it easier for Jan to communicate with us from the Great Beyond."

On the grave there was now a Czech flag as well as a photo of Welzl with a very broad grin on his face. It also had a box with notebooks filled with comments by Czech visitors. In the most recent notebook, I wrote the following comment in English: "May the gods of whimsy still be with you, Jan!"

ⵊⵏⵏⵏ

MEETING HELGI PJETURSS

I once met an Icelander named Helgi Pjeturss who'd been dead for nearly fifty years. I'll explain how I met him shortly, but first I'll mention that this fellow was perhaps Iceland's foremost twentieth-century geologist and an authority on rocks deposited by passing glaciers. He was also a grand mal eccentric who believed (among other things) that dreams are gifted to us earthlings by extraterrestrials, and that Icelandic is the language of the afterlife. Likewise, he believed that we spend much of that afterlife on other planets.

So, there I was, attending a seance sponsored by the Helgi Pjeturss Society in the Icelandic town of Kópavogur. Along with the female medium, there were eight of us seated in a circle and holding hands so that our energy would bond us together. An extremely scratchy LP recording of Vivaldi's *The Four Seasons* was playing on a phonograph at the far side of the room. The only light was a globe of the world illuminated by a single flickering light bulb.

The first person to pay us a visit was Helgi himself, who, being dead, was obliged to speak through the medium. Helgi welcomed us to the seance (he always comes first, I was subsequently told). He said he was currently hanging out on the planet Neptune and enjoying it enormously.

The next person was a deceased Italian geologist, a friend of Helgi's, who wanted to reassure Helgi that he was all right even though he had somehow gotten stuck in the Andromeda Galaxy. He said several other individuals also happened to be stuck along with him, including the German astronomer Johannes Kepler, who was an excellent conversationalist, and the medieval Icelandic bard Oddr Snorrason.

A short while later, the medium was speaking in the low, deep voice of . . . Abraham Lincoln. Honest Abe reported that he was still having a difficult time learning Icelandic, so he couldn't communicate very well with other afterlifers. He also wanted us to know that he didn't bear a grudge against John Wilkes Booth. Indeed, he'd played croquet with him just the other day, and Booth won two of their three games.

"Wasn't that nice?" one of the seance-goers remarked to me afterward. "The medium brought forth a fellow countryman of yours just because you were attending her seance."

Yes, it was nice, I had to agree. Especially nice since the medium could have brought forth a much less desirable president than Abraham Lincoln. But it was also an example of Icelandic hospitality, where a guest is treated with exceptional, often idiosyncratic kindness.

ꜱꜱꜱꜱ

A HEROINE OF THE ARCTIC

I would have much rather met Christiane Ritter than such male luminaries of Arctic exploration as Commodore Robert Peary, Sir John Franklin, and Adolphus Greely. Especially, I would rather have met her than Peary, who had the disposition of a corporate tycoon. "Mine at last!" he exclaimed upon reaching (or not reaching) the North Pole, as if he'd just engineered a hostile takeover.

Christiane was neither an explorer nor a luminary. She was an Austrian *hausfrau* who, prior to the year she spent in Norway's Svalbard archipelago, had never strayed far from her comfortable surroundings in central Europe. Yet perhaps because she had no interest in a goal like reaching the North Pole or traversing the Northwest Passage, she could appreciate the Arctic more than the aforementioned luminaries. And in appreciating the Arctic, indeed thriving in it, she gave the lie to the notion that women do not belong at the ends of the earth.

In 1934, thirty-six-year-old Christiane decided to join her hunter-trapper husband Hermann in Svalbard because she thought it would be a good place to (in her words) "read thick books in the remote quiet and, not least, sleep to my heart's content." Her friends were appalled: a woman's place was, if not in the home, at least not in a geography that lacked the usual amenities.

And their small hut at a locale called Gråhuken did lack amenities. Every known amenity. Stuck by herself in what she called "this small, bleak box" during an epic snowstorm, she nearly went crazy. But once the storm had passed, she realized that, however difficult the circumstances, she could survive them. And from then on, she didn't regard the Arctic as an adversary. Rather, it was a realm "where everything goes its prescribed way . . . without human intervention."

Christiane wrote a book, *Eine frau erlebt die Polarnacht* (translated into English as *A Woman in the Polar Night*), about her year in Svalbard. The book abounds with real-life epiphanies. For instance, she describes a landscape of "frozen splendor" whose clarity makes it seem worthy of a photograph. She reaches for her camera, then pauses and makes the following observation: "It seems to me a deadly sin to steal a piece of this supernatural scene and carry it away with me." She doesn't take the photograph.

A personal aside: I wish the obsessive camera-wielders of the contemporary world would emulate Christiane.

Do these folks actually see what they're photographing? Get rid of that bloody camera, I want to tell them, and use those twin orbs in your head commonly called eyes, lest they become vestigial.

After a year, she left what she called "the Arctic wilderness," never to return. But she didn't really need to return, since she brought that realm back with her— or at least she brought back a radically different way of looking at the world. Not long after she returned to Austria, her house burned to the ground, but rather than mourn its loss and the loss of almost all of her possessions, she felt grateful. For she could now live simply, without a surfeit of ballast, just as she'd lived in the hut in Gråhuken.

"A year in the Arctic should be compulsory to everyone," Christiane would say to her friends and family. "Then you will come to realize what's important in life . . . and what isn't."

⌐⌐⌐⌐

MEETING HALLDÓR LAXNESS

On my first visit to Iceland, I didn't know a single person, but I had read several novels by Halldór Laxness, so when I saw his name in the country's phone directory, I rang him up. I dare say most other countries don't have listings in their phone books for their Nobel Laureates.

Halldór (Icelanders are known by their first names) answered the phone. "You've read my novels?" he said with a sense of, it seemed to me, surprise. "Then please come to my house for a visit."

So it was that I took a bus from Reykjavík to Mosfellssveit, where Halldór lived. His wife Auður greeted me at the door. "Halldór is upstairs reading Proust," she told me, "and he'll be down shortly."

My encounter with Halldór was a lot more personal than my aforementioned encounters with Jan Welzl, Helgi Pjeturss, and Christiane Ritter. When he finally came down the stairs, I asked him whether he liked reading Proust.

"Not particularly," he said.

"Then why are you reading him?"

"Because my publisher requires it."

I was appalled. Here was the winner of a Nobel Prize in literature, an eighty-year-old man who'd written thirty or so books, and his publisher required that he read Marcel Proust. I wondered whether that publisher wanted him to inject a dose of French civility into his staunchly Icelandic oeuvre.

As it happened, my ears were less than perfectly attuned to Icelandic English. Halldór hadn't been reading Proust, but rather the *proofs* for his forthcoming book, a repudiation of the praise he gave to Stalin in a much earlier book, *Gerska æfintyrið* (*A Russian Adventure*).

I explained my error to him, then asked him why he didn't care for the writer Proust. "I'm not interested in the lives of upper-class French people," he told me.

"Me, I'm very fond of Proust," Auður said, pronouncing the word very slowly for my benefit.

Enough of Proust, I thought. I now mentioned to Halldór my delight in his well-known quote, "Nobody should be allowed to kill more people than he can consume himself."

"*Jæja*," he said, smiling at Auður. "She never cooks more than one or two persons at a time. If there's any meat left over, she puts it in the freezer."

"But *luda* [halibut] is a much better food than us humans," Auður added.

I changed the subject again. "It's really a shame you're not better known in America," I said.

"I am not Agatha Christie!" he exclaimed, clenching his fist. Then, as if to prove this point, he lit one of the large cigars that were his trademark in Iceland. After he smoked most of the cigar, he put the rest of it in a pipe and smoked it, thus indicating that a genuinely creative individual can smoke a good cigar right down to the final ash.

⌐⌐⌐

A RARIFIED BALLAD

In 1986, I visited Stewart Letto, a singer of traditional songs in L'Anse au Clair in southern Labrador.

"You're from the Boston area?" he said to me. "I happen to be a big Red Sox fan."

Indeed, the Red Sox were currently playing the New York Mets in the World Series, and he turned his television onto mute so he could watch game six while he was singing old songs to me. The announcers began mouthing silently like demented fish.

At one point Stewart was singing a ballad about an Elizabethan sea battle that, according to nineteenth-century English folklorist Sabine Baring-Gould, was no longer sung in England. It was still being sung in Labrador—by Stewart.

In the midst of singing this rare ballad, Stewart shouted, "Oh, shit!" For his television had just showed the infamous ground ball trickling through Red Sox first baseman Bill Buckner's legs, an error that paved the way to the Red Sox losing the World Series.

Some years later I donated the tape of Stewart singing this ballad to the Labrador Institute in Goose Bay.

It's possible that some future listener to this tape will hear the exclamation of "Oh, shit!" and think those words are actually part of the four-hundred-year-old ballad, possibly an indication that the bad guys (i.e., the Spaniards) were winning the sea battle.

ﾍﾍﾍﾍ

MURDERED BY A MADMAN

In the cemetery on Siberia's Wrangel Island, I noticed a lone Star of David among several rows of Russian orthodox crosses. A Russian scientist named Sergei was researching the mammoths who'd once lived on Wrangel, and he seemed to be knowledgeable about the island's history, so I asked him whether he knew who might be buried below the Star of David.

"Dr. Nikolai Lvovich Vulfson," Sergei said. "A Jewish doctor murdered by a madman." Whereupon he told me this story.

Vulfson, Wrangel Island's doctor in the mid-1930s, was a highly altruistic person. The "madman" was the island's governor, Konstantin Semenchuk, a very unaltruistic person. Vulfson looked after the sick at all hours of the day and night, while Semenchuk made remarks like this: "Up here I am everything. I have all the rights, including shooting people."

Not surprisingly, these two individuals had some unpleasant interactions. Semenchuk told Vulfson repeatedly not to give medical care or even food to the island's small Yupik population. "For if you give those beasts any sort of care, they will become lazy and turn against us," he declared, adding, "Then we will have to shoot them . . ."

On December 26, 1934, Vulfson learned about a possible typhoid outbreak in the distant Yupik village of Mys Florens. The doctor immediately set off for the village by dog team, accompanied by Stepan Startsev, a dog team driver and Semenchuk's trusted subordinate. The sled arrived at its destination without Vulfson. "The Jew wandered off in a blizzard," Startsev remarked nonchalantly, although there was no evidence of a blizzard.

On January 4, 1935, Vulfson's bullet-riddled body was found lying in the snow. A suicide, Semenchuk said.

Vulfson's widow didn't believe her husband's death was a suicide and radioed for a government investigation. An inspector arrived and began collecting information that determined Semenchuk was responsible for Vulfson's death. "Shoot the *zhyd*!" he had said to Startsev. The inspector also determined that Semenchuk had raped a large number of the young Yupik girls on the island. With Startsev, Semenchuk was recalled to Moscow.

At Semenchuk's trial by the Soviet Supreme Council, the prosecutor called the governor "human waste" who should be executed as soon as possible. Semenchuk protested. He was a citizen of Mars, he said, and thus he wasn't subject to the same rules as a typical Soviet citizen. The court did not buy this defense. It sentenced Semenchuk and Startsev to death for "banditry and violation of Soviet law." Shortly thereafter, they were both executed by a firing squad.

After finishing the story, Sergei offered me this personal admission: "People like Semenchuk and Startsev, they're why I prefer mammoths to human beings."

∿∿∿∿

A CHAT ABOUT EVIL SPIRITS

On an unusually hot day in the village of Uelen, Chukotka, I was talking with a Russian ethnographer named Dmitri.

"The Chukchi who live here once burned the dried roots of the angelica plant [*Angelica archangelica*] to keep evil spirits out of their *yarangas* [tents]," Dmitri told me.

"What sort of evil spirits?" I said, mopping the sweat from my brow.

"Family members who didn't know they were dead. They just stuck around the *yaranga*, breaking dishes and making loud screams at night. The smoke from burning angelica roots would get rid of them."

"Wouldn't the dead family member get angry at a living family member who's trying to get rid of him or her?"

"Sometimes, *da*. So, the best way to protect yourself against angry dead people is to carry around a raven's claw at all times."

"I'll remember that," I said, mopping more sweat from my brow. Then I asked him if there were any evil spirits besides deceased family members.

"Yes, *keedles*," he said. "These were six-legged invisible polar bears that break into the *yarangas* and try to eat people. Especially, they liked to eat young children. But the Chukchi don't believe in *keedles* anymore. Now they believe in kindles, *ha ha* . . ."

"Any more evil spirits nowadays?" I inquired.

"Yes, there's a really bad one," he observed, mopping his own sweat now. "The heating up of our planet, and even the burning of an angelica root won't get rid of it . . ."

ᶺᶺᶺ

SOME LIKE IT HOT

On a visit to Tasiilaq, East Greenland, I saw plastic Hawaiian leis in the village's shops and a fisherman who was wearing an ultralight "Aloha" T-shirt even though the temperature was just below freezing. Fortunately, he was wearing a parka beneath the T-shirt.

One evening I went to a concert by a traditional singer I knew from previous visits to Greenland. In the concert, the woman sang mostly Hawaiian songs, including several Hawaiian reggae songs, while her boyfriend accompanied her on an electric guitar.

At the end of the concert, there was a loud burst of applause. The woman bowed to the audience and shouted "Aloha!" at them.

As it happened, the T-shirts, leis, and music were moonbeams from a larger lunacy. I met the woman the following day, and she told me China was flooding Tasiilaq with Hawaiian bric-a-brac in order to make locals believe the melting of Greenland's ice (it's losing 267 billion metric tons of ice a year) will turn the island into a tropical paradise.

"If we like what's happening to our land, the Chinese think we'll *really* like what they plan to do with that land once it's melted," the woman said.

"They plan to mine it to death," her boyfriend declared angrily. "They don't want just oil, they also want gold, nickel, zinc, and iron. *Aqaa avanigut!* I just wish they would leave us alone!"

I asked them if they actually had any interest in Hawaiian songs. "I would much rather sing traditional Greenlandic songs," the woman said, "but most of our people, especially the young ones, they only want to hear Hawaiian songs."

"And I'd much rather play a fiddle or hit a *qilaat* [frame drum] than play an electric guitar," her boyfriend added, the anger in his voice now replaced by sadness.

Later I went into a store and asked a Greenlander working there whether he had any *angmagssat panertut* (dried capelin). *Angmagssat* is a fish in the smelt family that gave the town of Tasiilaq its former name of Angmagssalik.

"*Nagga*," the fellow replied, shaking his head. "People aren't interested in eating it anymore."

"How about some *arfivik* [smoked whale meat] then?" I asked.

He shook his head again, then as I left the store, he grinned at me and said, "All-ew-ah," which sounded like "Hallelujah" but was really his mispronunciation of aloha.

Once outside, I gazed at the melting landscape around me and wondered how soon it might be before this part of Greenland would be called "the Oahu of the North."

ᴨᴨᴨᴨ

THE ULTIMATE SOCIAL DISTANCER

He read Jane Austen, smoked his pipe, wrote in his journal, and stoked his Primus stove. Every few hours, he would venture outside—or try to venture outside—in order to gauge the winds. Augustine Courtauld was 150 miles from the nearest other person, a distance that makes the COVID-19 social distancing mandate of five or six feet seem like a veritable hug. He remained at this epic distance for more than five months.

The twenty-six-year-old Courtauld was a member of the 1930 British Arctic Air Expedition, whose purpose was to find a place on the Greenland ice cap for transatlantic planes to land and refuel. Based in the village of Angmagssalik (now Tasiilaq), the expedition set up a small station on the ice cap to determine whether the winter weather would or would not be too vehement for planes.

Courtauld offered to occupy the station by himself. All but one of his colleagues thought it was madness for him to live alone in such a remote place. The one exception was explorer J. M. Scott, who subsequently wrote that Courtauld's desire to situate himself on the ice cap was "no more complicated than why people want to go exploring."

In December 1930, Courtauld's so-called quarantine began. His home was a tent whose only ventilation was a pipe two inches in diameter protruding from the tent's apex. His provisions consisted of kerosene, paraffin, a bottle of cod liver oil, two bottles of concentrated lemon juice, oatmeal, pemmican, chocolate, tobacco, tea, and a bunch of novels. Needless to say, he had no means of contacting the outside world.

Day after day, he was obliged to dig through the snow that blocked the tent's tunnel so he could go outside and get weather measurements. Icicles of condensation hung from the tent's roof and dripped on his face as well as onto his increasingly uncomfortable sleeping bag. The tent sagged ominously under the weight of the snow, threatening to collapse. If it did collapse, his life would come to an end shortly.

Weeks passed, and blizzards raged continuously. A six-day blizzard blocked the tent's entrance, and thus Courtauld could no longer crawl outside to look at the weather instruments. Much of his paraffin leaked away, and thus he could use his stove only for cooking, not for heating. Ice choked the ventilation pipe, preventing fresh air from entering the tent. His feet ended up becoming frostbitten. Also, he ran out of tobacco for his pipe and was obliged to smoke dry tea leaves.

You might think he would have gone stark raving mad. But his journal informs us otherwise. Here are a few brief entries:

"Beastly weather. Finished *Guy Mannering*. Jolly good book!"

"My end shall be peaceful enough . . . and I have four bars of chocolate to eat during it."

"[The] curious growing feeling of security . . . came over me as time passed."

To what can we attribute his seemingly Zen-like attitude? Being a dyed-in-the-wool Englishman, albeit one with a distant French Huguenot background, his typically English stiff upper lip may have contributed to this attitude. But he also realized (as he put it in his journal) that focusing on danger can make that danger much worse.

Having twice been driven back to the coast by gale force winds, Courtauld's dogsled rescue party at last arrived at the station on May 5, 1931. They searched for the tent, but it was buried by snow. At last they saw the ventilator pipe barely sticking up out of the snow.

"Are you all right?" the expedition's leader, Gino Watkins, shouted into the pipe. To which Courtauld replied: "Yes, I'm perfectly fit," adding, "I'm frightfully sorry to have given you so much trouble."

When the rescue party dug through the snow and located him, he did seem fit, although somewhat thinner and his beard more matted than when they had last seen him. On the lengthy sled trip back to Angmagssalik, he spent most of his time reading Alexander Dumas's *Count of Monte Cristo.*

Once he returned to civilization, Courtauld received an enormous amount of something he disliked far more than being frostbitten—namely, attention. Asked questions about his ice cap overwintering by the media, he would quickly come up with an exit line, such as, "Sorry, but I must go now and meet my nanny," or he would respond in a laconic manner.

He was especially laconic in his interview with King George VI, who awarded him the Polar Medal:

The King: I am sure you were very cold, Mr. Courtauld?
Courtauld: No sir.
The King: You were hungry though?
Courtauld: No sir.
The King: You must have felt desperately lonely?
Courtauld: No sir.
The King: I am happy to give you the Polar Medal.

As for myself, I never met Courtauld, who died in 1959, but I did meet an elderly Danish man in Angmagssalik in 1985 who'd had a brief conversation with him shortly after he returned to the village.

"What did he tell you?" I asked the man eagerly.

"He said the ice cap was a great place to catch up on one's reading," the Danish man replied.

⎍⎍⎍⎍

CODA: WIND BLASTED

In Kulusuk, East Greenland, a fifty to sixty mile-per-hour gale once blew my tent flat against the tundra. I resurrected the tent, but the huffing, puffing, ferocious wind blew it down within a few minutes. I resurrected it again, and it blew down yet again.

At last I moored down flaps with some rocks, and the tent now seemed content to remain standing, although it also seemed to protest this upright posture by making constant snapping and cracking sounds.

A short while later, a local seal hunter dropped by for a visit. I gave him one, two, three cups of coffee, since no Greenlander can survive on a single cup. I had a package of dehydrated beef stroganoff, and the man gazed curiously at the bag.

"You can have some of it if you want," I said, handing him the bag.

He immediately put some of the powder in his mouth, then grimaced. "American food no good," he said.

We sat in the tent to escape the wind, but we could hardly hear each other talking because it was almost as noisy inside as it was outside thanks to the wind. At one point a powerful blast brought down the tent's heavy white canvas on top of us. I cursed mightily, but the Greenlander laughed, then laughed some more. A time-honored method among northern indigenous people for dealing with circumstances considerably more serious than a fallen tent.

As I write these words almost twenty years later, COVID-19 and its multiple variants have the planet in a metaphoric stranglehold. I can imagine both the Greenlander my tent had fallen on and this book's initial encounter, the hundred-year-year-old Vuntut Gwich'in woman Annie Henry, responding to that stranglehold in the same way—by laughing. In doing so, they would escape the fear and trembling inspired by the virus and perhaps even triumph over the virus itself by boosting their immune systems. After all, laughter is the best medicine.

ACKNOWLEDGMENTS

I'd like to thank the following individuals for aiding and abetting the journeys I've described in this book: Aleleke, Sarah Baikie, Randy Bell, Kim Cheechoo, Gernot Dick, Kelsey Eliasson, Thröstur Eysteinsson, Fred Ford, Bill Gawor, David Gluns, Jack Kiviaq, Paul Kroeger, Peter Lesniak, Randy Letto, Stewart Letto, Ted Mala, Jimmy Mianscum, John Michel, Leah Otak, Tshinish Pasteen, Nolan Peterson, Uinipapeu Rich, Umgy Riskov, Doris Saunders, Mary Sears, Boris Shostelsky, Sven-Erik Svendson, John Trapper, Wanagan, and Lene Zachariessen.

I'd like to thank Emily Schuster for being such a savvy copyeditor, Sarah Nawrocki for being such a splendid managing editor, and Trinity University Press director Tom Payton for eagerly taking on this book.

LAWRENCE MILLMAN is a writer, Arctic explorer, and mycologist who has made more than forty expeditions to the Arctic and subarctic. He has taught at the University of Iceland, the University of New Hampshire, Tufts University, and the University of Minnesota. His eighteen books include *Last Places*, *At the End of the World*, *Fungipedia*, *Our Like Will Not Be There Again*, *Hiking to Siberia*, *Northern Latitudes*, and *Goodbye, Ice*. His work has appeared in *National Geographic*, *Smithsonian*, *Sports Illustrated*, *Outside*, *Atlantic Monthly*, the *Walrus*, the *Sunday Times* (London), and *Orion*, among other publications. He has received a Guggenheim Award, a Fulbright Fellowship, and a Lowell Thomas Award. When not on the road or in the bush, he lives in Cambridge, Massachusetts.

CPSIA information can be obtained
at www.ICGtesting.com
Printed in the USA
JSHW020817170123
36224JS00001B/1

9 781595 349859